Mentals 1

Alan McSeveny Rachel McSeveny Diane McSeveny-Foster

Introduction

Using the Mentals Books

Each unit of a Mentals Book is programmed to review content from the previous two units of the Student Books. For example, Signpost Mentals Book Unit 5 can be used to review Signpost Student Book Units 3 and 4 while the Student Book Unit 5 is being taught. Unit 5 from both books should be completed in the same week.

Presentation

- The content of the strands Number and algebra, Measurement and space, and Statistics and probability is revised.
- Essential number skills and language are given a high profile. These will appear in most units.

ID cards

- The ID cards on pages 4 and 5 review important terms addressed at Year 1 level.
- These cards can be used over and over again to improve and consolidate understanding.

Mixed-topic questions

The units present questions in a mixed-topic format.

- This is essential for thorough understanding and continuous review.
- It will allow the teacher to discover weaknesses that could otherwise pass unnoticed.
- The approach reflects real life – similar questions do not often occur together.
- It provides a real test of understanding.

If you do not use a Student Book

This book will be invaluable to those who do not use a Student Book, as it ensures both thorough coverage and constant review of the syllabus content.

Multiple-choice questions

The multiple-choice questions on page 70 introduce a variety of question types.

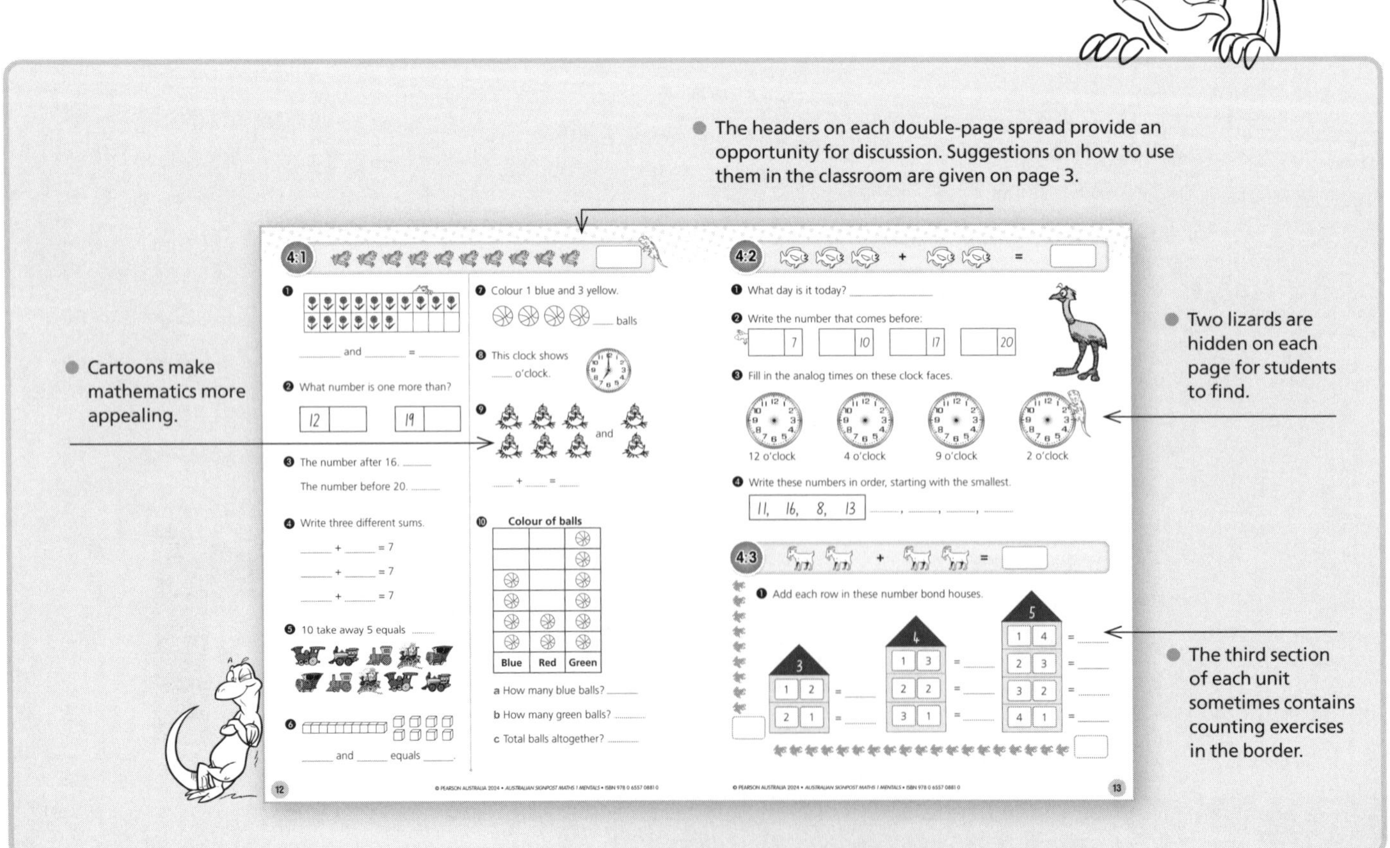

1 Contents

Unit header activities

1:1 Count the tomatoes. (Q1)
2:1 Count the scooters. (Q4, 10)
3:1 Count the triangles.
4:1 Count the frogs.
5:1 2 + 8
6:1 5 + ___ = 6
7:1 Count by tens. (Q7)
8:1 Count by tens.
9:1 6 – 2 (Q1)
10:1 4 + 7 (Q1, 5)
11:1 5 + 4 (Q7, 8)
12:1 Which holds the most? (Q9)
13:1 Number line addition (Q1)
14:1 Number line addition (Q1)
15:1 Name and describe 2D shapes.
16:1 Number line subtraction (Q6)
17:1 Number line subtraction (Q6)
18:1 Months of the year (Q3, 6)
19:1 Describe 2D shapes. (Q2, 7)
20:1 3 + 5 (Q11)
21:1 3 + 7 (Q12)
22:1 Write the numbers modelled. (Q2)
23:1 Number pattern (Q5)
24:1 Number pattern (Q1, 5)
25:1 Number patterns (Q1, 5, 6)
26:1 Number pattern (Q8)
27:1 2D shapes (Q3, 7)
28:1 3D objects (Q6)
29:1 6 – 3
30:1 Circle the heavier sides.
31:1 Number pattern
32:1 Slide or reflection? (Q3)

1:2 Count the beetles.
2:2 Count the horses.
3:2 Count the circles.
4:2 3 + 2
5:2 Count the boats.
6:2 4 + ___ = 6
7:2 How many tens? (Q1, 2)
8:2 How many tens? (Q1, 3)
9:2 8 – 5
10:2 4 + 5
11:2 Count by tens. (Q1)
12:2 8 – 3 (Q3)
13:2 8 – 5
14:2 Count the squares.
15:2 Write the numbers modelled.
16:2 Numbers 1 to 6
17:2 Double 2. (Q2)
18:2 Double 3.
19:2 7 – 4
20:2 2D shapes 3 + 3 + 3
21:2 5 – 3
22:2 3 + 3 + 3 (Q1)
23:2 4 groups of 3 (Q2)
24:2 2 groups of 4
25:2 Months of the year (Q2, 3)
26:2 Count by tens from 5. (Q3)
27:2 Count by twos.
28:2 Months of the year (Q1)
29:2 Months of the year (Q1)
30:2 Describe 3D objects.
31:2 Bridging to tens (Q1)
32:2 Bridging to tens (Q1)

1:3 Numerals 1–10 (Q1)
2:3 Count the strawberries. (Q1)
3:3 Numerals 11–20
4:3 2 + 2
5:3 O'clock times
6:3 3 + ___ = 6
7:3 3 and 2 makes 5.
8:3 How many tens?
9:3 10 and 4 (Q1)
10:3 5 + 4 (Q1)
11:3 Write the numbers modelled.
12:3 Write the numbers modelled.
13:3 10 – 4
14:3 2 + 6 = 6 + 2 (Q1)
15:3 10 – 3 (Q1)
16:3 Name and describe 2D shapes.
17:3 Double 10. (Q1)
18:3 2 + 3 (Q1)
19:3 Pattern: 3, 6, 9, 12
20:3 4 + 6 (Q1)
21:3 4 + 3
22:3 6 + 4
23:3 Count by fives. (Q1)
24:3 Groups of 2
25:3 Pattern: numbers 1 to 5
26:3 Name and describe 2D shapes.
27:3 4 groups of 5
28:3 Count by twos. (Q1)
29:3 Groups of 2
30:3 Count by twos.
31:3 7 + 8
32:3 Count by fives.

ID card A

Do not write on this card.

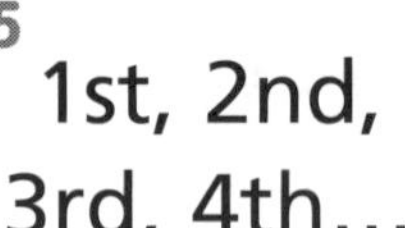

1	2	3	4	5
 a______	 s______	= is e______ to	 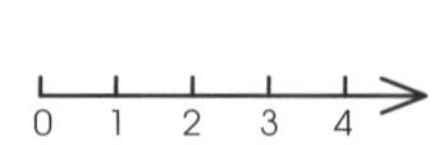 n______ line	1st, 2nd, 3rd, 4th… o______ numbers
6	**7**	**8**	**9**	**10**
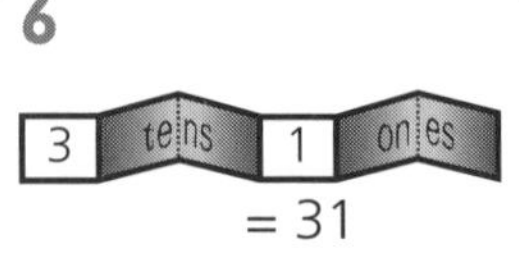 n______ expander	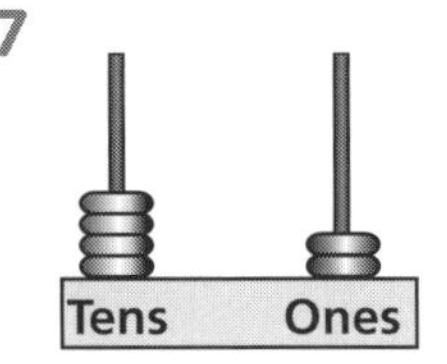 a______	 o______ b______	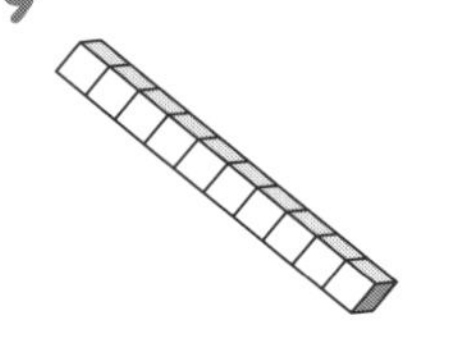 t______ b______	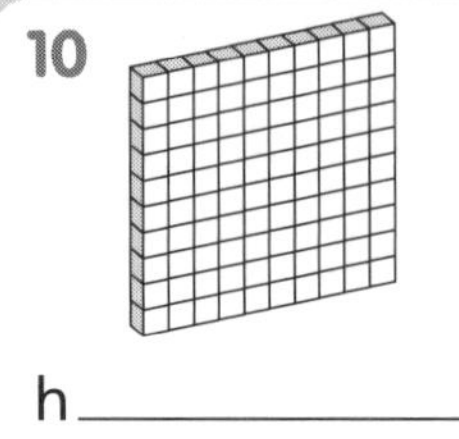 h______ b______
11	**12**	**13**	**14**	**15**
 d______	 c______	  ______ coin	  ______ coin	  ______ coin
16	**17**	**18**	**19**	**20**
______ coin	 ______ coin	 ______ coin	 ______ note	 ______ note
21	**22**	**23**	**24**	**25**
 ______ note	 ______ note	 ______ note	 Summer Autumn Winter Spring s______	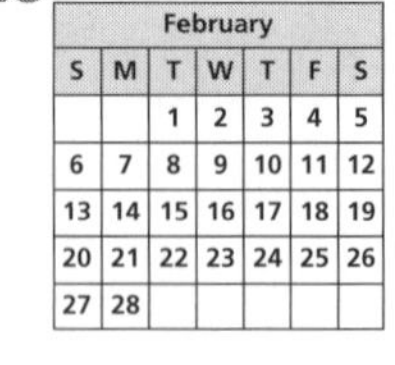 c______
26	**27**	**28**	**29**	**30**
 d______ time	analog clock  o'______	analog clock  h______ p______	analog clock  q______ p______	analog clock q______ t______

See page A1 for answers.

ID card B

Do not write on this card.

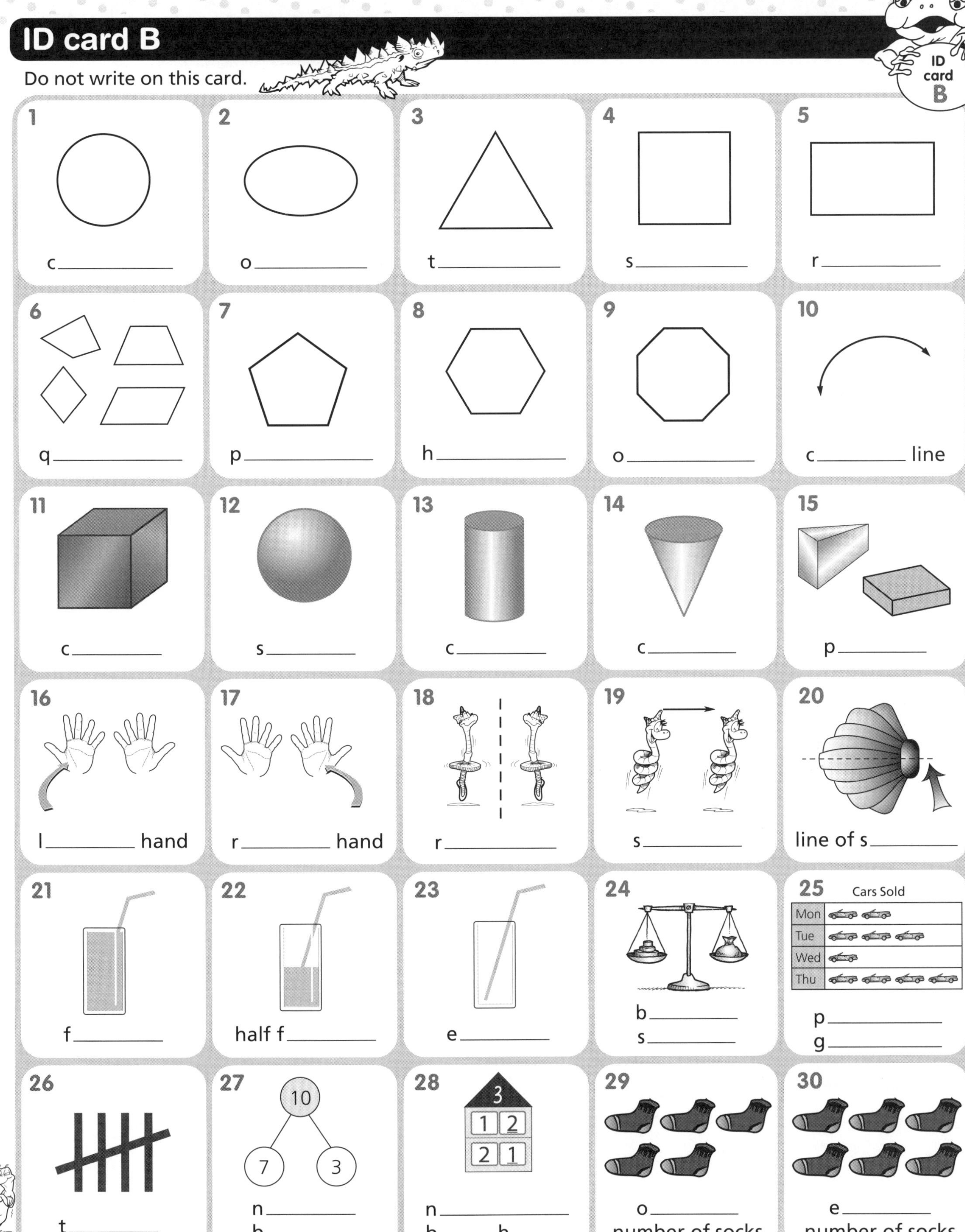

See page A1 for answers.

 AUSTRALIAN SIGNPOST MATHS 1 MENTALS • ISBN 978 0 6557 0881 0

1:1

1. How many leaves? ______

2. ☆☆☆☆

◯◯◯◯◯◯◯

There are ______ more circles than stars.

3. The day after Sunday is

______________________________.

4. Circle the one that holds the most.

5. 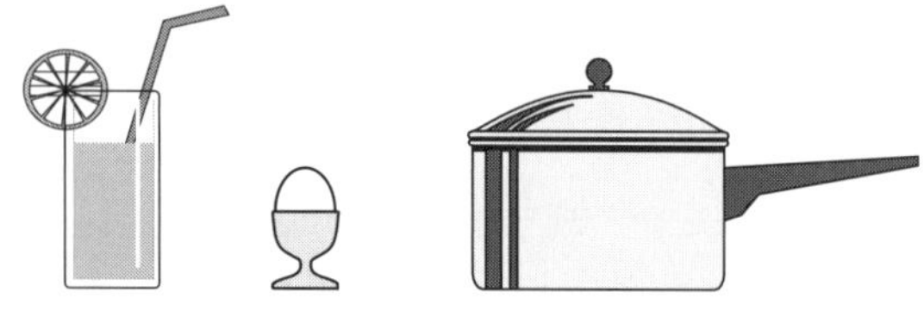

makes ____ pins.

6. The number after 5 is ______.

The number before 8 is ______.

7. 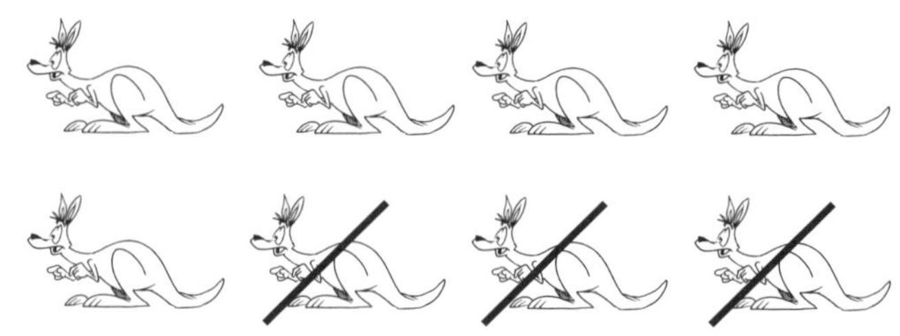

______ take away ______

is equal to ______.

8. Circle the group with the least.

9. Circle the heavy things.

10. Write the missing numbers.

a 2, ____, 4, 5, ____, ____

b 10, 9, 8, 7, ____, ____

11. Draw another object with straight edges.

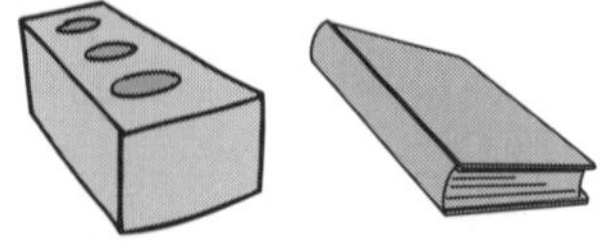

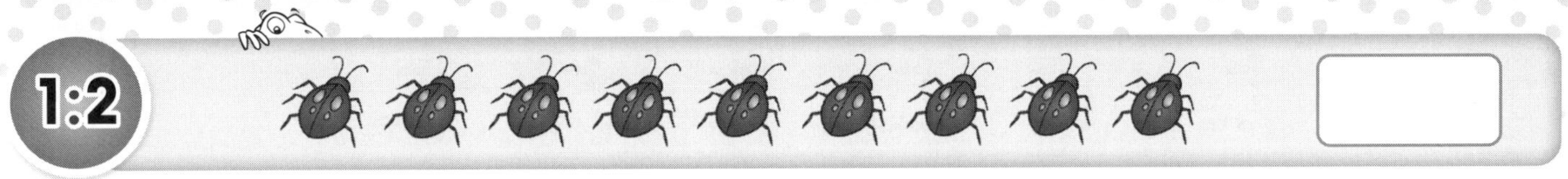

1:2

1 Ten lollipops, five fell on the ground.

How many are left? ____

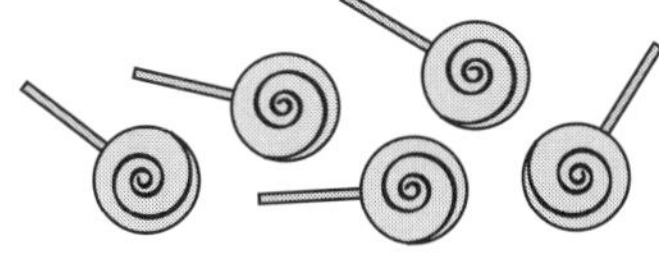

2 Colour 3 red and 2 blue.

____ fish

3 Draw pictures to complete the problem.

3 circles and 6 circles makes ____ circles.

1:3 1 2 3 4 5 6 7

1 Trace, then write each word. Draw shapes in each rectangle to show the number.

three three

eight eight

six six

2:1

❶ Trace and copy.

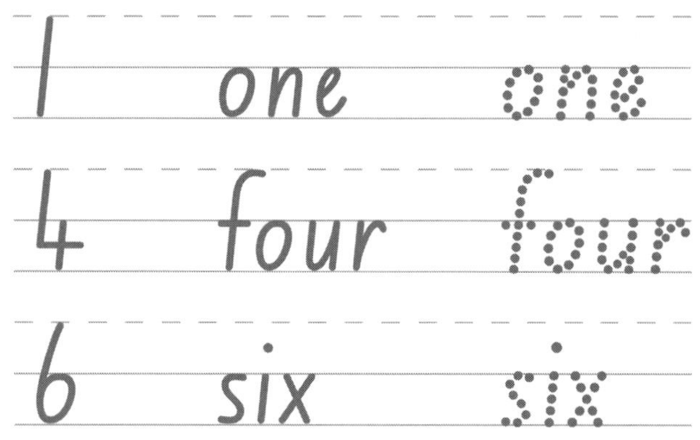

❷ The number before 4 is ____.

The number after 7 is ____.

Write the number ten. ____

❸ Name this shape.

____

❹ Cross out 18 hearts.

❺ 12, 11, 10, ____, ____, ____

❻ Write the numbers in order, from smallest to biggest.

a 4, 8, 2, 6

____, ____, ____, ____

b 7, 6, 8, 5

____, ____, ____, ____

❼ Eight fish, three swam away.

How many are left? ____

❽ 16, ____, 18, ____, 20

❾ The day after Monday.

____

❿ Draw 3 squares.

2:2

❶ Match:

six eight one ten two

8 6 10 2 1

❷

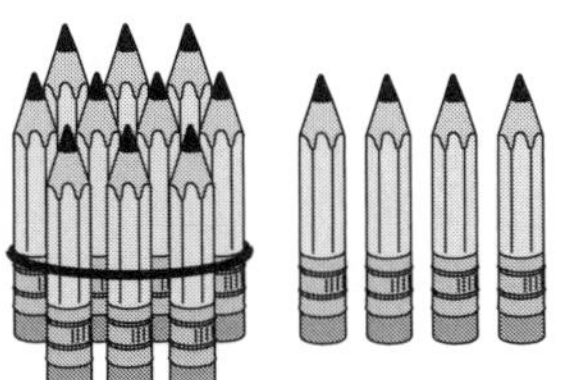

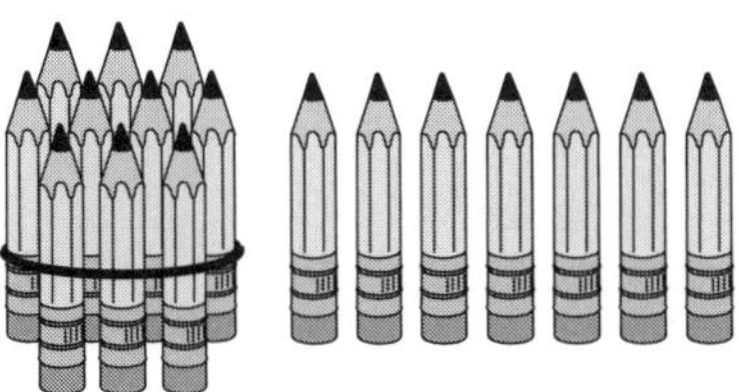

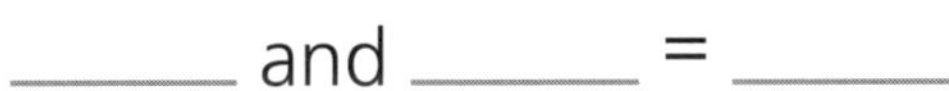

_____ and _____ = _____ _____ and _____ = _____

❸ Write these numbers in order, starting with the smallest.

12, 10, 13, 11

_____, _____, _____, _____

2:3

❶ Trace, then write each word. Draw shapes in each rectangle to show each number.

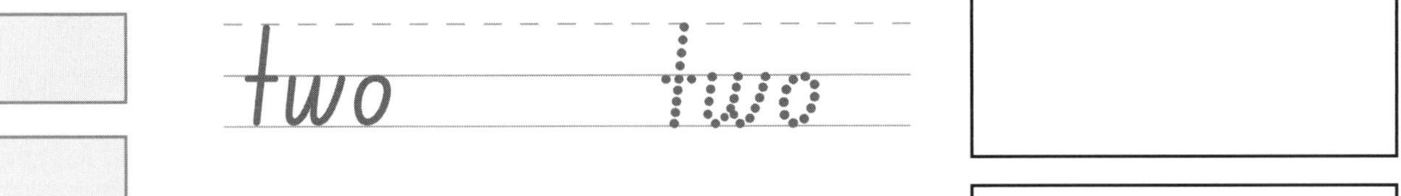

two two

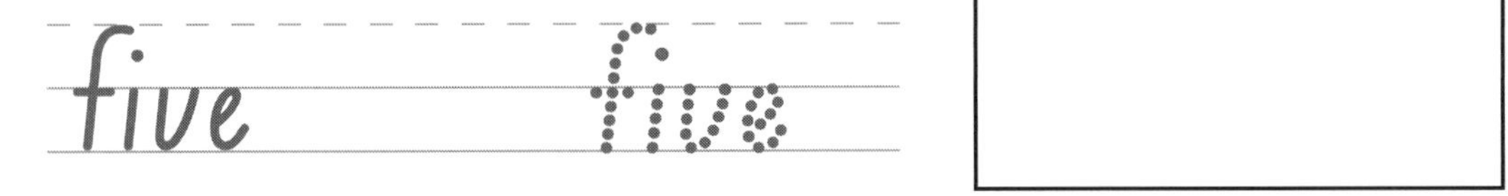

five five

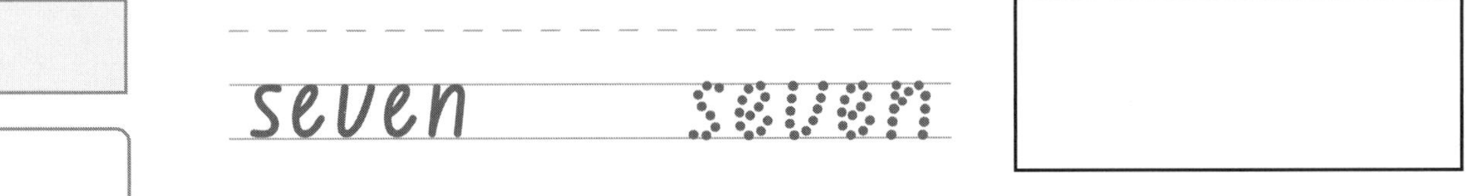

seven seven

 • *AUSTRALIAN SIGNPOST MATHS 1 MENTALS* • ISBN 978 0 6557 0881 0

❶ What comes before 8? ____

❷ Colour to show 17.

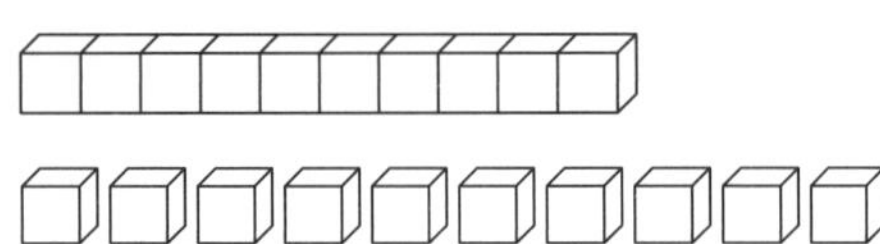

❸ Colour 3 milkshakes pink and 2 milkshakes yellow.

How many milkshakes are coloured? ____

❹ **Pets**

Scott	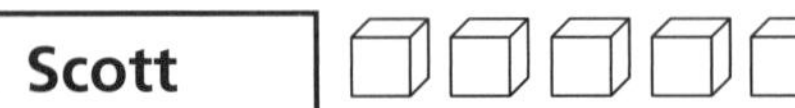
Kate	
Christie	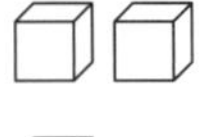
Greg	

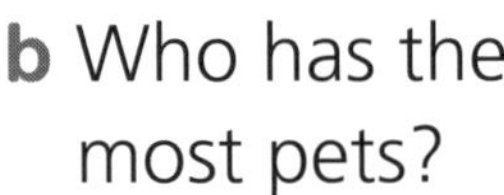

a How many pets altogether? ________

b Who has the most pets? ________

c Who has the least pets? ________

d How many more pets than Kate does Scott have? ________

❺ Write the missing numbers.

11, 12, ____, 14, ____, ____, ____, 18, ____, ____

❻ Finish this pattern.

△ 8 △ 8 ____ ____

❼    and 

____ and ____ makes ____.

$3 + 2 =$ ____

❽ Circle the objects that are easy to lift.

❾ Write three different sums.

____ and ____ makes 4.

____ and ____ makes 4.

____ and ____ makes 4.

 • *AUSTRALIAN SIGNPOST MATHS 1 MENTALS* • ISBN 978 0 6557 0881 0

3:2

1. Match each number with its name.

3 4 5 2 7

four three five seven two

2. Write the missing numerals.

0, ___, ___, 3, ___, ___, 6, ___, ___, ___, ___, ___, ___, ___

3. Count on by ones. 15, 16, ___, ___, ___, ___, ___, ___, ___

4. Count back by ones. 20, 19, ___, ___, ___, ___, ___, ___, ___

5. How many days in one week? ___

3:3

11 12 13 14 15 16 17 18 19 20

1. Count the shaded squares and complete.

a 

10 and 4 makes ___.

b 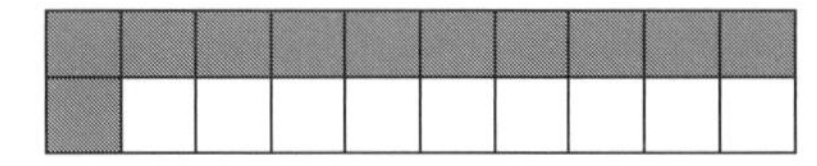

10 and 1 makes ___.

c 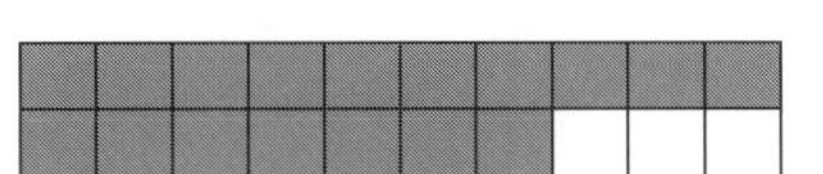

10 and 7 makes ___.

d 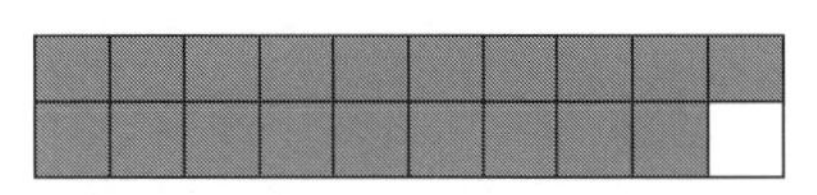

10 and 9 makes ___.

e 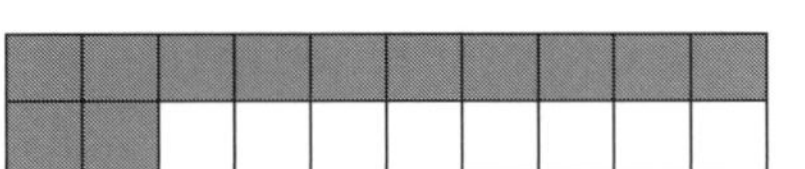

10 and 2 makes ___.

f 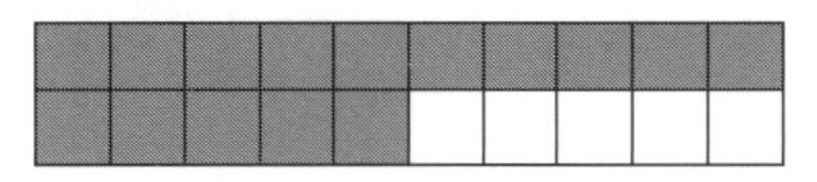

10 and 5 makes ___.

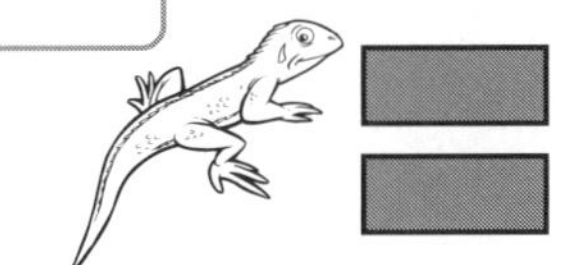

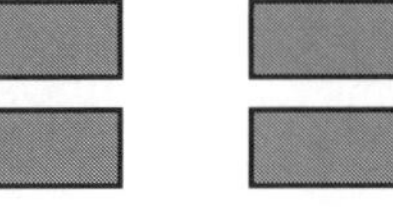

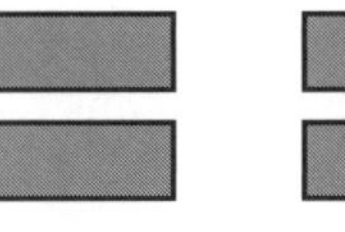

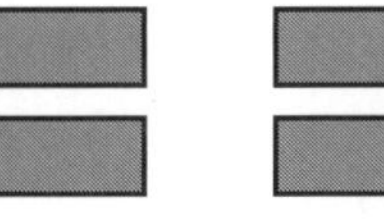

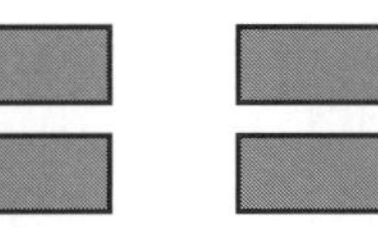

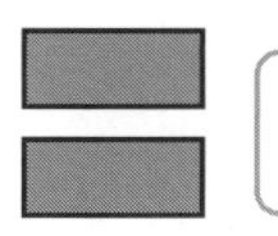

 • *AUSTRALIAN SIGNPOST MATHS 1 MENTALS* • ISBN 978 0 6557 0881 0

❶

_______ and _______ = _______

❷ What number is one more than?

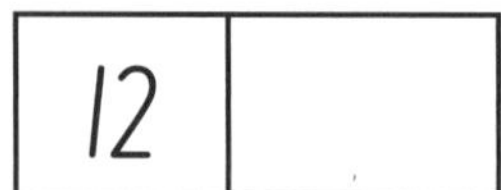

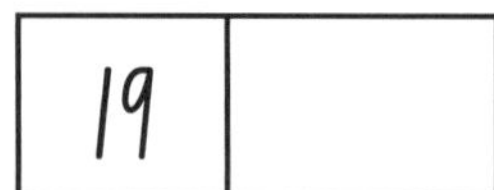

❸ The number after 16. _____

The number before 20. _____

❹ Write three different sums.

_____ + _____ = 7

_____ + _____ = 7

_____ + _____ = 7

❺ 10 take away 5 equals ____.

❻

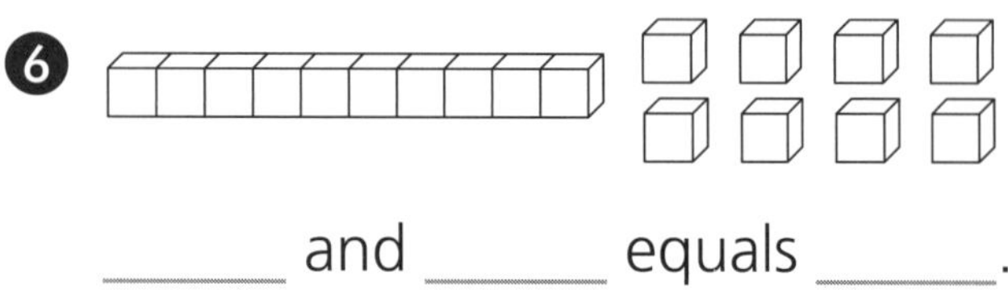

_____ and _____ equals _____.

❼ Colour 1 blue and 3 yellow.

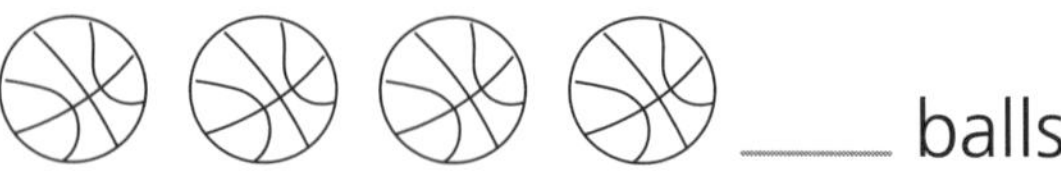

____ balls

❽ This clock shows

____ o'clock.

❾

and

____ + ____ = ____

❿ **Colour of balls**

Blue	**Red**	**Green**

a How many blue balls? _____

b How many green balls? _____

c Total balls altogether? _____

 • *AUSTRALIAN SIGNPOST MATHS 1 MENTALS* • ISBN 978 0 6557 0881 0

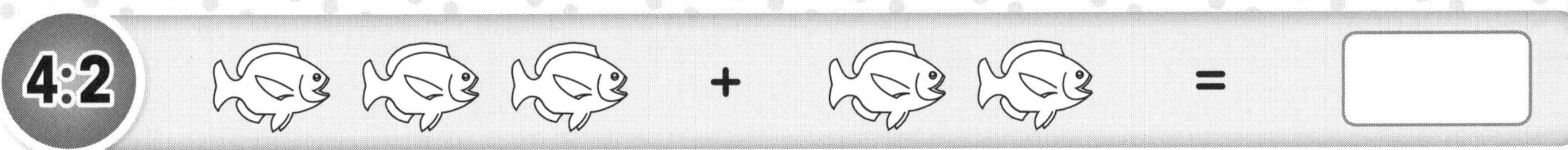

❶ What day is it today? ____________

❷ Write the number that comes before:

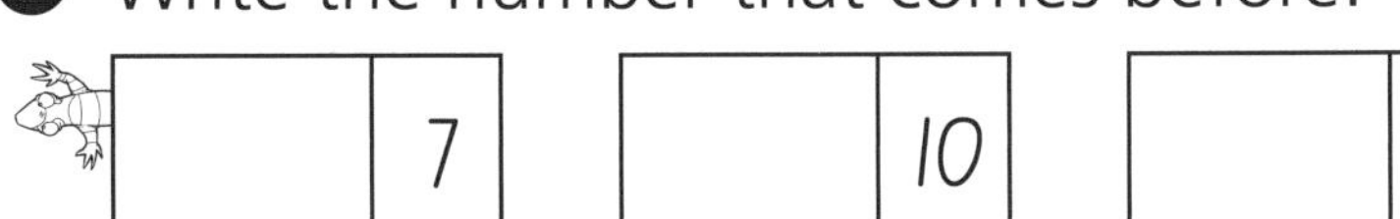

❸ Fill in the analog times on these clock faces.

12 o'clock

4 o'clock

9 o'clock

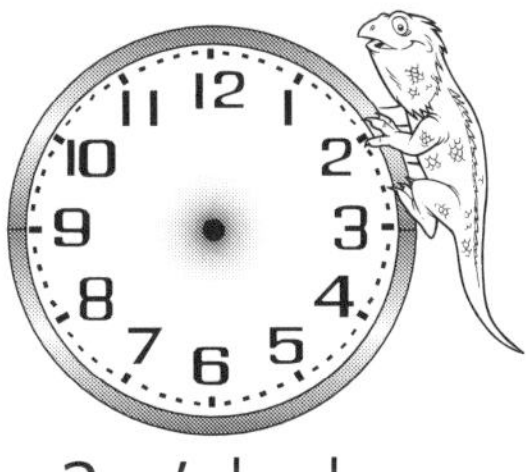
2 o'clock

❹ Write these numbers in order, starting with the smallest.

11, 16, 8, 13

____, ____, ____, ____

❶ Add each row in these number bond houses.

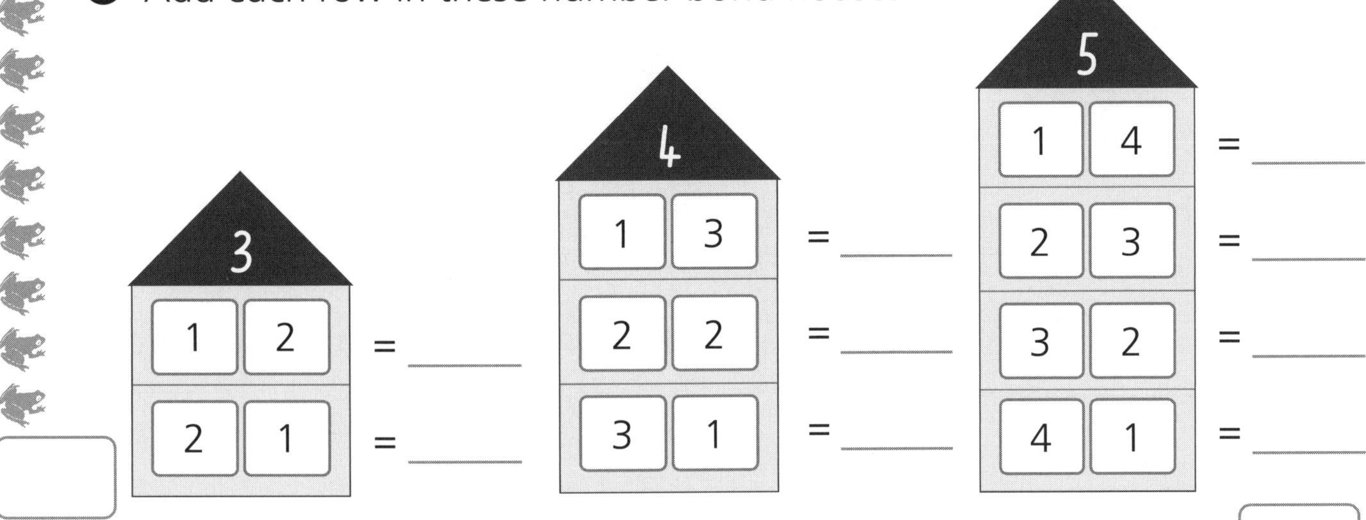

5:1

  +        = ____

1. The number after 17. ____

   The number after 14. ____

2. What is the time?

____ o'clock ____ o'clock

3. Fill in the missing numbers.

   14, ____, 16, ____, 18

4. Write three different sums.

   ____ + ____ = 9

   ____ + ____ = 9

   ____ + ____ = 9

5. Write the numbers in order, from smallest to biggest.

   a 7, 9, 1, 5

   ____, ____, ____, ____

   b 8, 3, 6, 2

   ____, ____, ____, ____

6. Count back by ones.

   17, 16, ____, ____, ____

7. 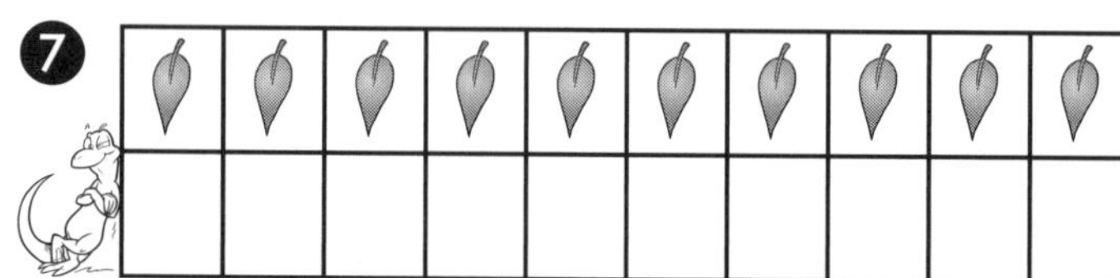

   10 and 2 is ____.

   10 and 3 is ____.

   10 and 5 is ____.

8. Write the missing numbers.

	13	

	8	

9. Estimate, then count the number of marbles.

   Guess = ____

   Count = ____

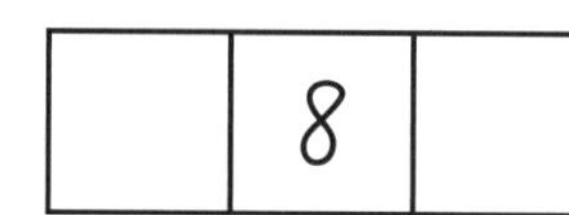

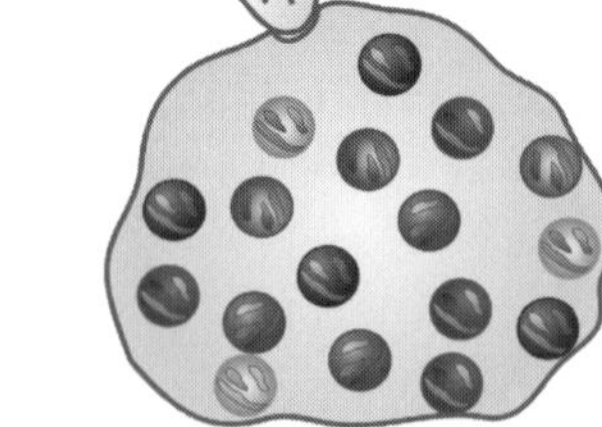

10. Draw a triangle to the left of this square.

 ISBN 978 0 6557 0881 0

boats

❶ Write the missing numbers.

		3				7		9	10
11					16			19	20

❷ Write these numbers in order, starting with the smallest.

12, 10, 13, 11

_____, _____, _____, _____

❸ Complete each tower so the two numbers add to 10.

9	6	5	3	1	8	2	4

❶ Add each row in these number bond houses.

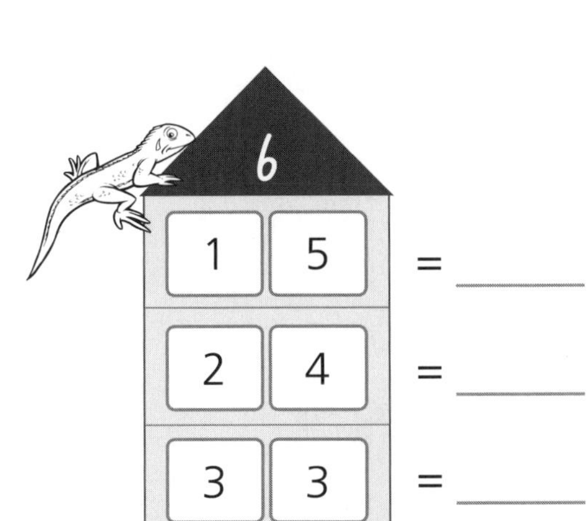

7
1 6 = _____
2 5 = _____
3 4 = _____
4 3 = _____
5 2 = _____
6 1 = _____

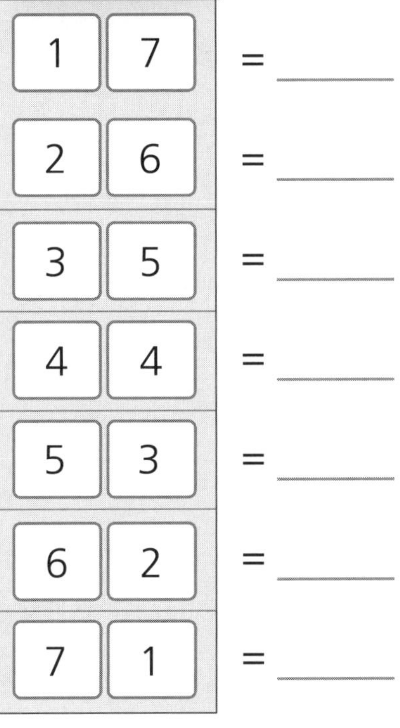

  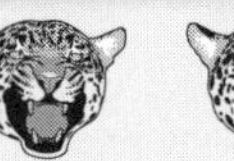   / 

5 + ☐ = 6

❶ Count back by ones.

12, 11, 10, ____, ____,

____, ____, ____

❷ Complete each tower so the two numbers add to 10.

6	9	4	5

❸ Match the shapes and objects.

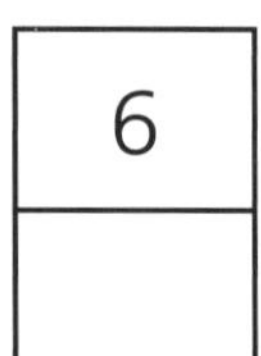 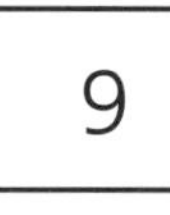 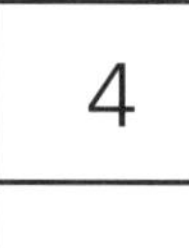

 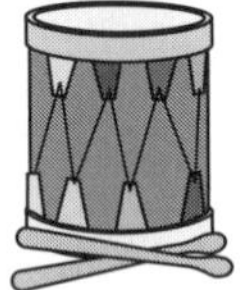 

❹ 

Circle.

The woman is:

to the **right** / **left** of the man,

behind / **in front of** the trolley.

❺ 4 + 5 = ____ 5 + 3 = ____

3 + 4 = ____ 6 + 2 = ____

❻ Join the dots to finish the shape.

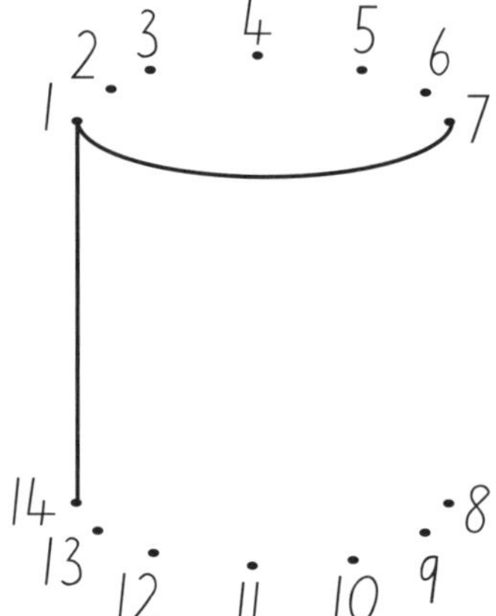

❼ 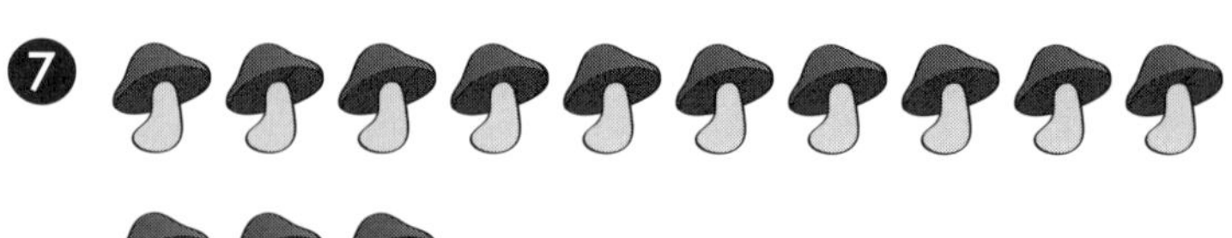

10 and ____ makes ____.

10 + ____ = ____

❽ Use lines to match the foods to the 3D objects.

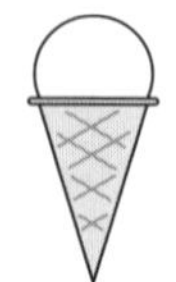 

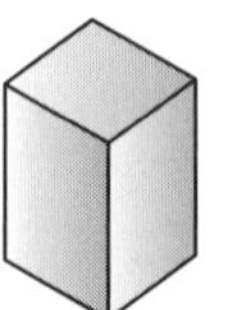 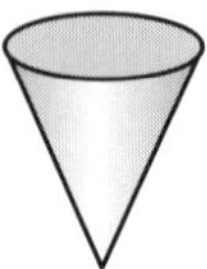 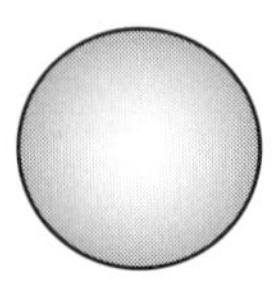

 • *AUSTRALIAN SIGNPOST MATHS 1 MENTALS* • ISBN 978 0 6557 088 0

❶ Draw one cow **inside** the paddock.

Draw two birds **above** the tree.

Draw a dog **next to** the tree.

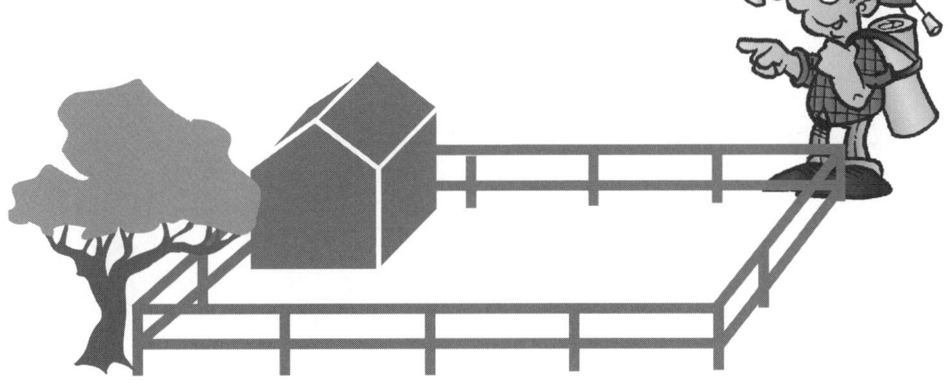

❷ 0 + 5 = ____ 7 + 3 = ____ 6 + 3 = ____ 4 + 3 = ____

6 + 2 = ____ 5 + 5 = ____ 3 + 2 = ____ 2 + 8 = ____

❸ Write these numbers in order, starting with the smallest.

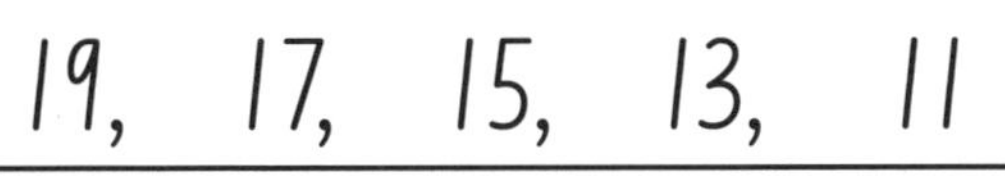

____, ____, ____, ____, ____

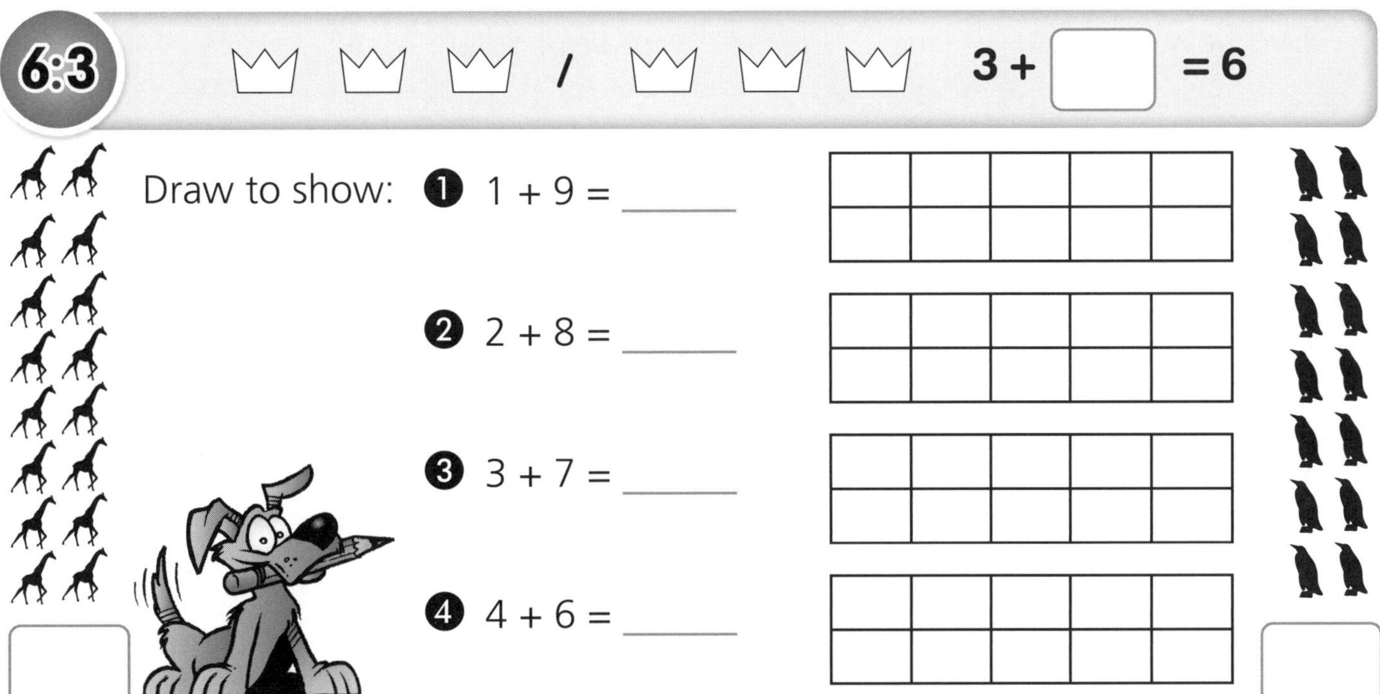

7:1 ten, twenty, thirty, forty, fifty, sixty, seventy, eighty, ninety

1 3 + 2 = ____ 6 + 4 = ____

8 + 3 = ____ 9 + 5 = ____

2 Add a number to give each tower a total of 10.

5	4	9	7

3 How many ones blocks would be the same length as the tens block?

____

4 Five owls.

Two flew away.

How many are left? ____

5 The pencil is ____ paperclips long.

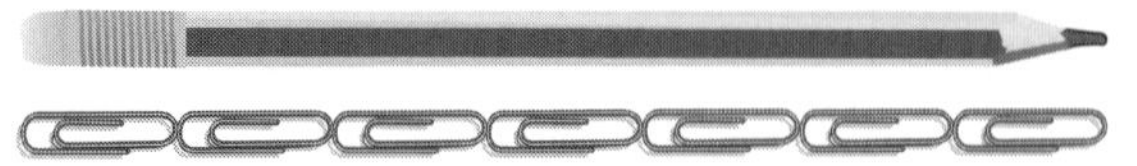

6 Match the shapes.

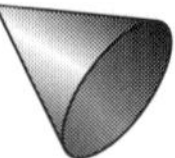  

7 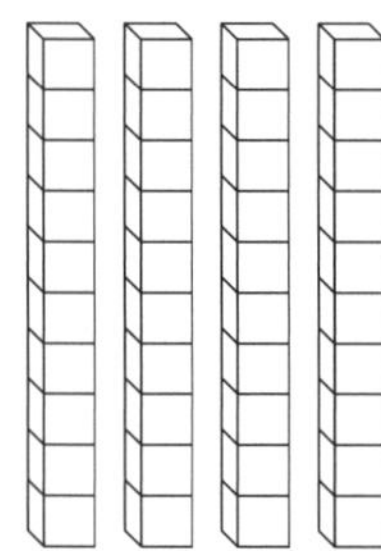

____ tens

This number is

____ .

8 Circle things longer than your ruler.

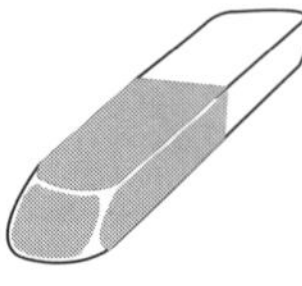 

 ISBN 978 0 6557 0881 0

7:2

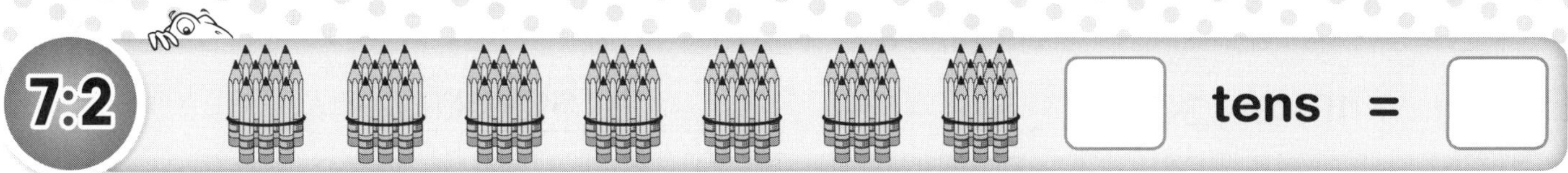

❶ 10, 20, 30, ____, ____, ____, ____, ____, ____, ____

90, 80, 70, ____, ____, ____, ____, ____, ____, ____

❷ Write the missing tens numbers.

a 40, ____, 60, ____ **b** ____, 80, ____

❸ Match each question to its answer. Use counters if you need help.

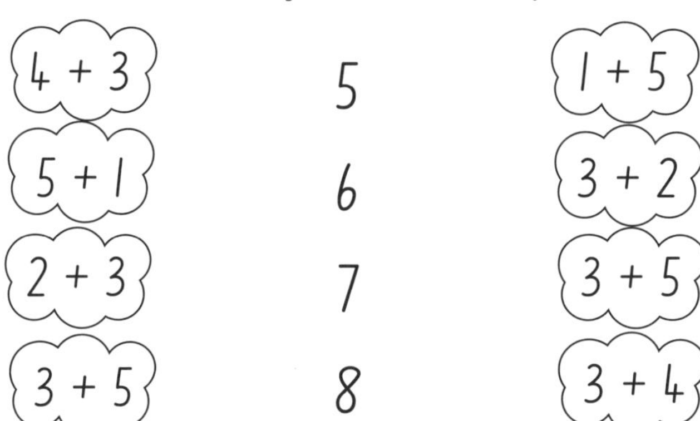

❹ Join the dots to make a picture.

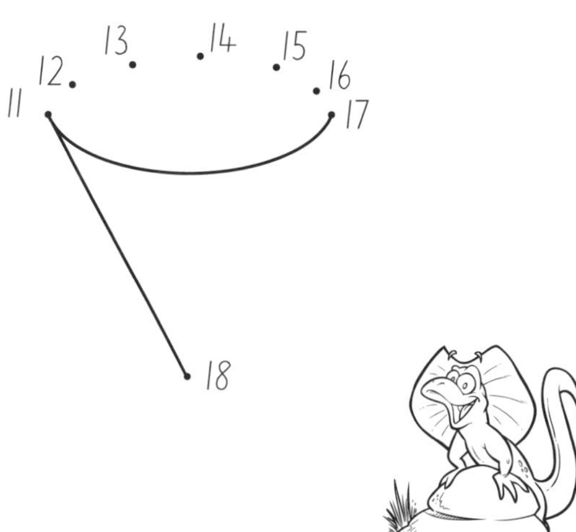

7:3

☆☆☆ **and** ☆☆ **makes** ☐ **stars.**

❶ Complete each number bond house. Each row adds to make the number at the top of the house.

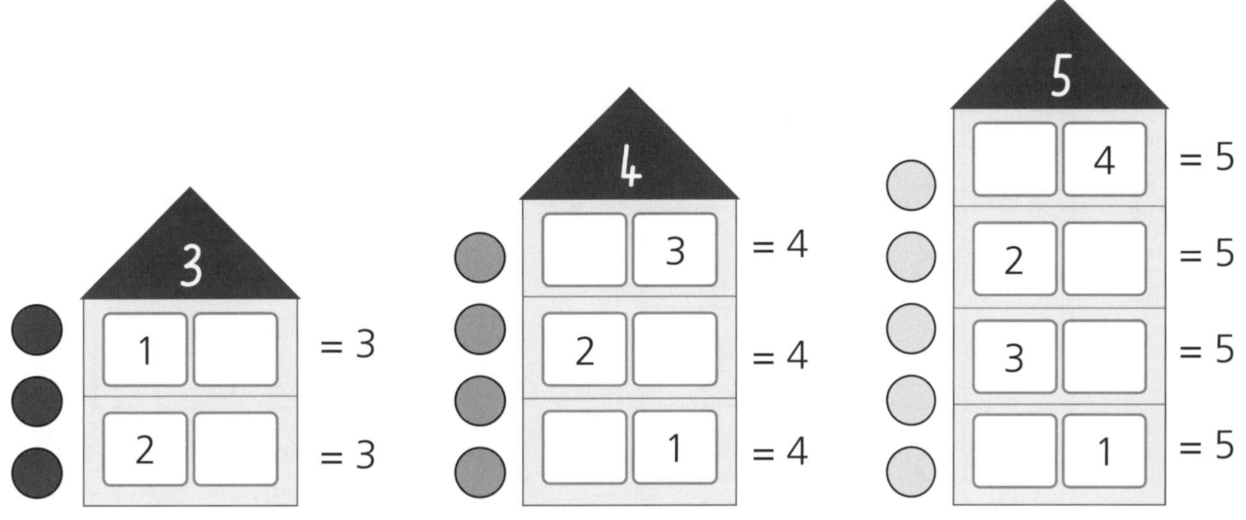

8:1 10, 20, 30, 40, ____, ____, ____, ____, ____, ____

❶ Write the word for:

30 ________________

60 ________________

❷ Colour the longer pencil.

❸

10 – 4 = ____

❹ Fill in the missing numbers.

4		6	7	8	9
14		16	17		19
	25		27	28	
34		36	37		39
44		46			49
	55	56	57		59

❺ How many erasers would be the same length as the pencil? ______

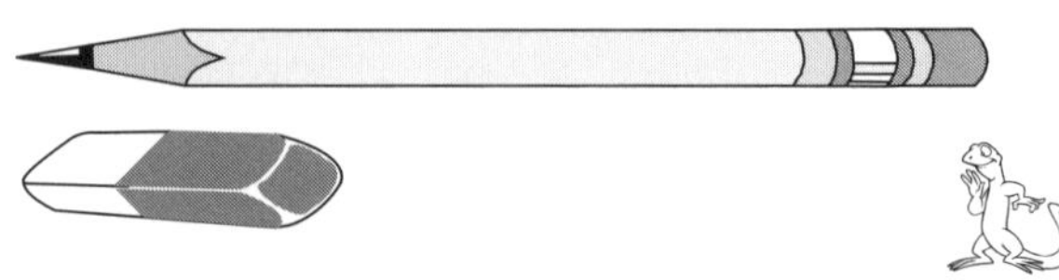

❻ 5 + 5 = ______ 7 + 3 = ______

8 + 2 = ______ 3 + 4 = ______

4 + 4 = ______ 4 + 6 = ______

1 + 9 = ______ 3 + 3 = ______

❼

9 subtract 3 = ________

❽ Write the number after:

a 22 ______ **b** 50 ______

Write the number before:

c 83 ______ **d** 70 ______

❾ Write these numbers in order, starting with the smallest.

56, 81, 37, 73

______, ______, ______, ______

❶ Circle 3 tens.

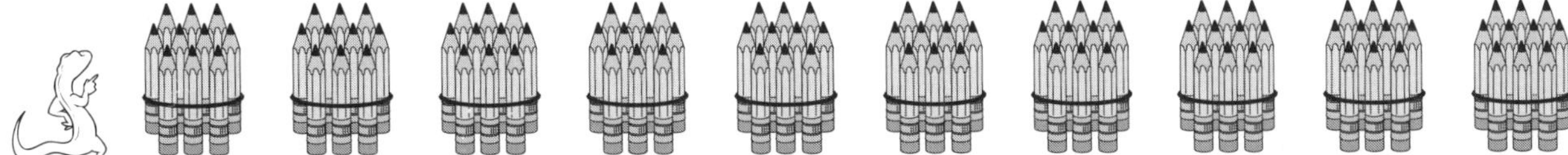

❷ Match the names and numerals.

80 30 50 90 60

fifty thirty eighty ninety sixty

❸ Estimate how many birds. Circle groups of ten, then count.

Estimate = ________ Count = ________

Groups of ten = ________

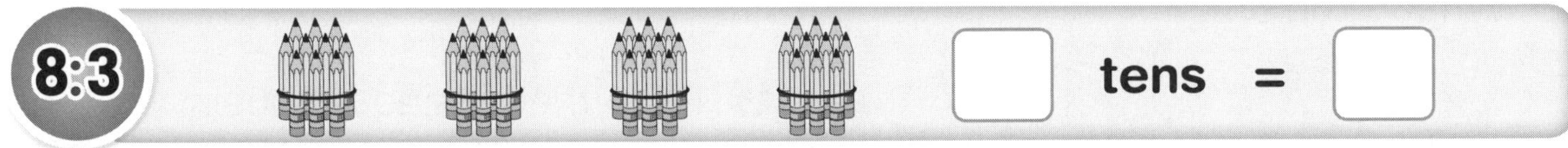

❶ Complete each number bond house. Each row adds to make the number at the top of the house.

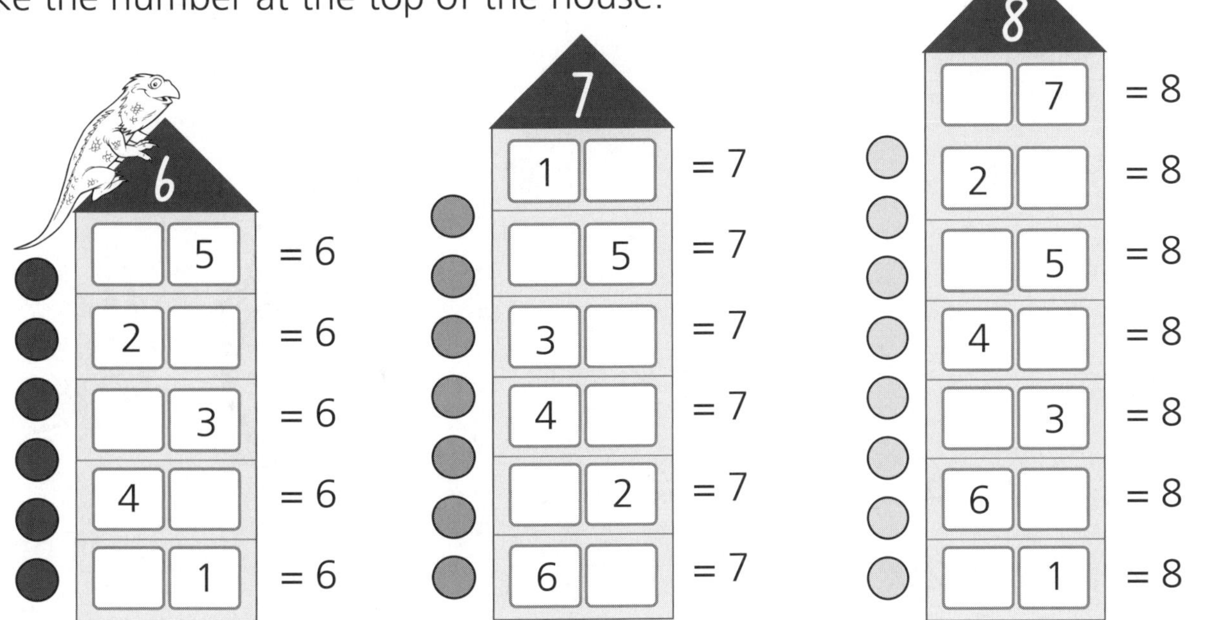

© PEARSON AUSTRALIA 2024 • *AUSTRALIAN SIGNPOST MATHS 1 MENTALS* • ISBN 978 0 6557 0881 0

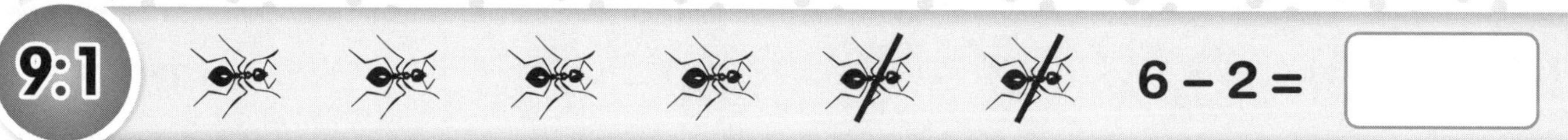

❶ Eight bananas, three eaten.
How many are left? ____

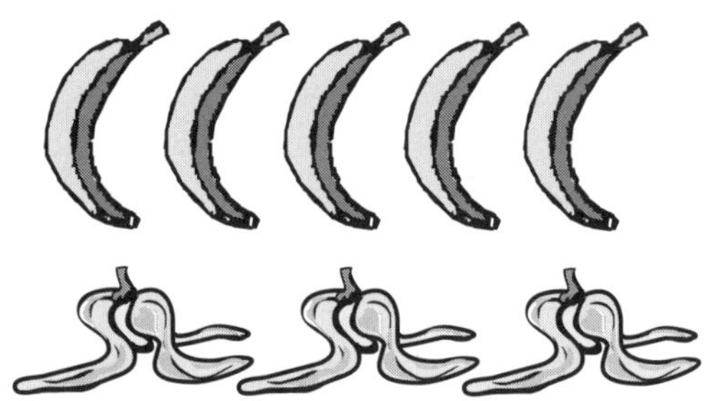

❷ How many blocks would be the same length as the pencil? ______

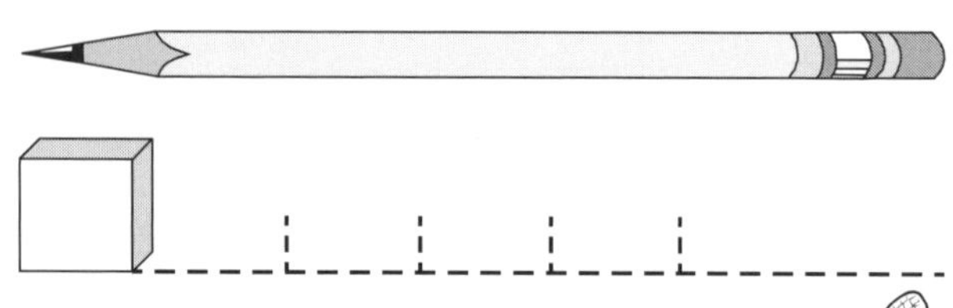

❸ What is the time?

____ o'clock ____ o'clock

❹ 8 + 2 = ____ 6 + 4 = ____

❺ Complete:

a 14, ____, 16, ____, 18

b 22, ____, 20, ____, 18

❻ Write odd or even, then write the number.

a **b**

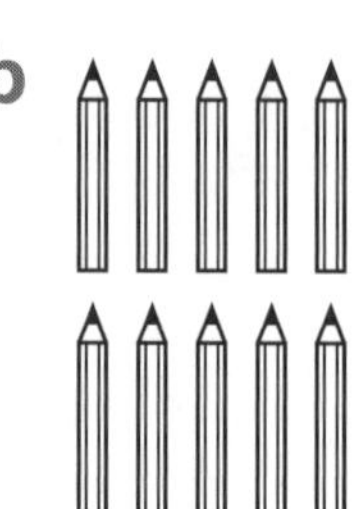

____________ ____________

____________ ____________

❼ 

7 circles and 6 squares

7 + 6 = ________

❽ Fill in the missing numbers.

62	63			66	
	73		75		77

❾ Show these times.

a

half past 8

b

half past 2

 • *AUSTRALIAN SIGNPOST MATHS 1 MENTALS* • ISBN 978 0 6557 0881 0

1. Write the missing positions.

1st ______ ______ 4th ______

2. Fill in the missing numbers.

60		62		64	65		67	68	
	71		73	74		76		78	79
80			83	84		86	87		89
		92	93		95		97	98	

3. 90, 80, 70 ______, ______, ______, ______, ______, ______, ______

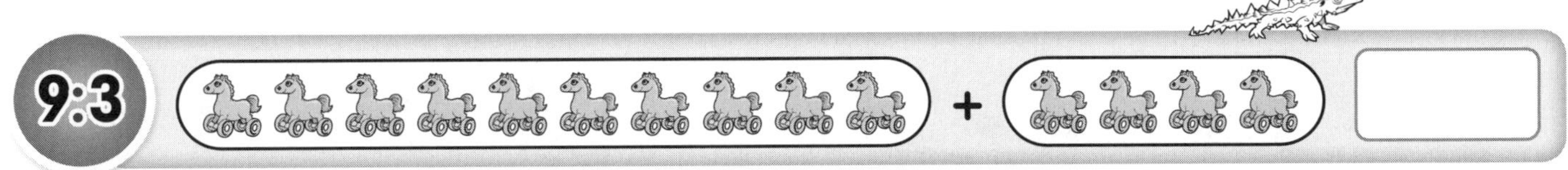

1. Use these pictures to answer the questions.

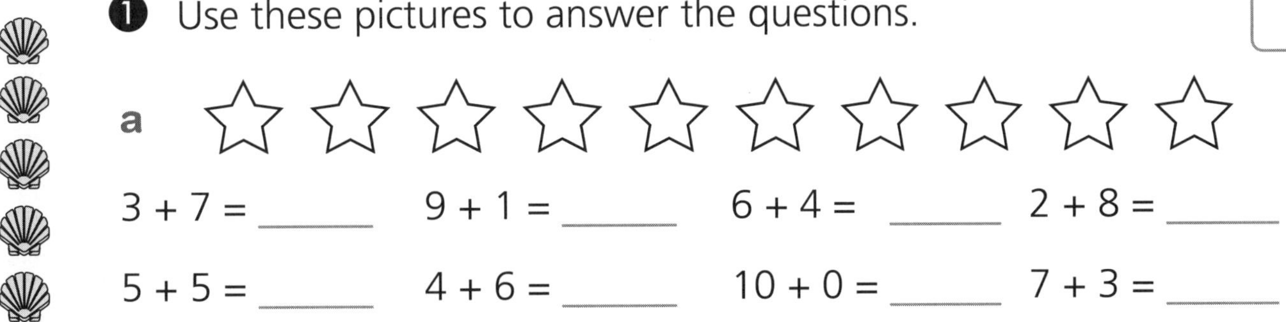

a

3 + 7 = ______ 9 + 1 = ______ 6 + 4 = ______ 2 + 8 = ______

5 + 5 = ______ 4 + 6 = ______ 10 + 0 = ______ 7 + 3 = ______

b

2 + 6 = ______ 1 + 7 = ______ 4 + 4 = ______ 3 + 5 = ______

8 + 0 = ______ 5 + 3 = ______ 6 + 2 = ______ 7 + 1 = ______

10:1

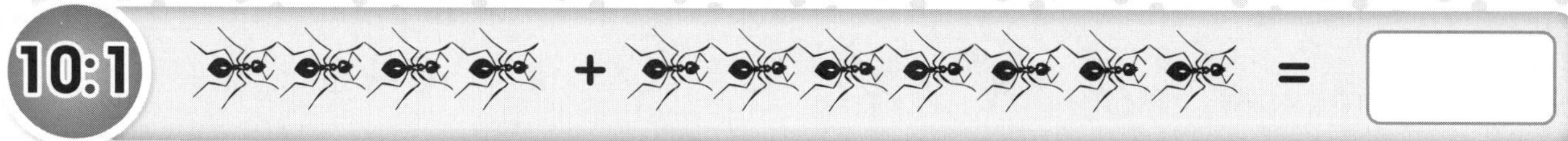

❶ 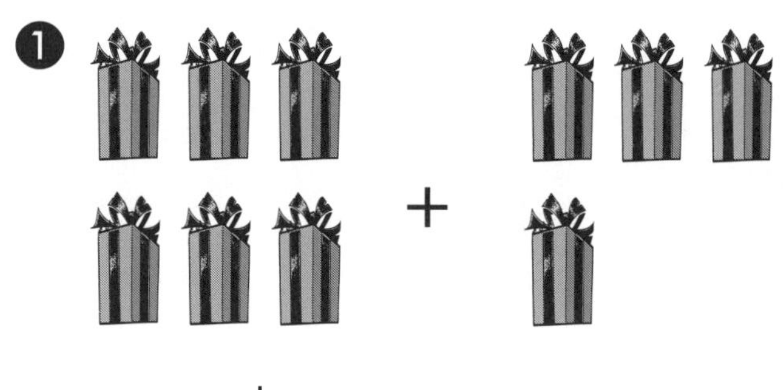

_____ + _____ = _____

❷ 

____ trees altogether

take away ____

is equal to ____.

❸ Write odd or even, then write the number.

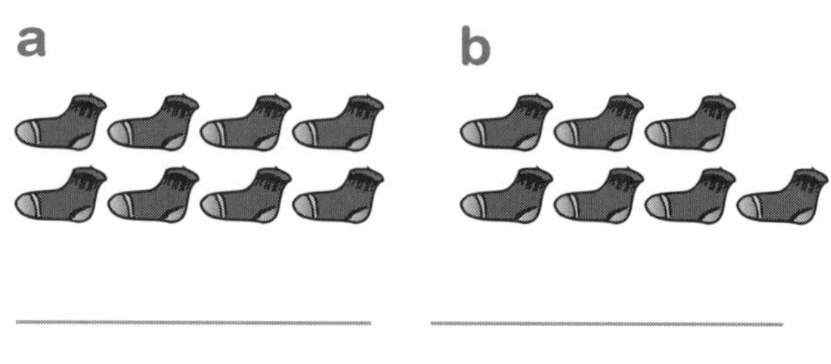

a ______________ **b** ______________

______________ ______________

❹ This time is

______________________.

This time is

______________________.

❺ 9 rectangles and 7 triangles

9 + 7 = _____

❻ Count on to find:

5 + 3 = _____ 6 + 2 = _____

4 + 2 = _____ 7 + 3 = _____

❼ Write the numeral for seventy. _____

❽ Write the time shown:

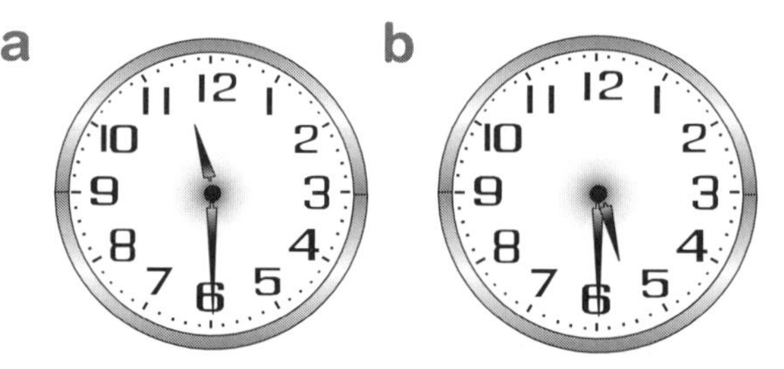

a half past ☐ **b** half past ☐

❾ Show a quarter past 5 on the clock.

❿ Show a quarter to 7 on the clock.

10:2

❶

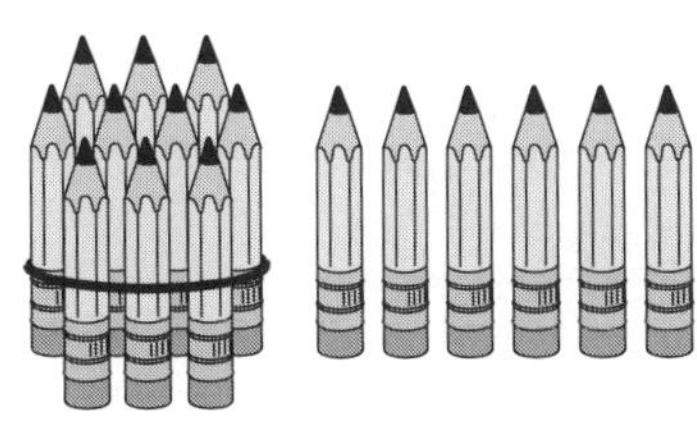

_____ and _____ = _____   _____ and _____ = _____

❷ Show each analog time.

half past 7

a quarter past 6

a quarter to 9

a quarter to 2

❸ 10, 20, 30, _____, _____, _____, _____, _____, _____, _____

90, 80, 70, _____, _____, _____, _____, _____, _____, _____

10:3

❶ **a** Start at  4 count on  I get to 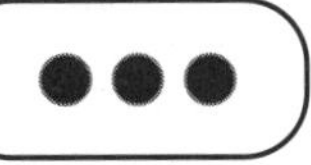

b 13 + ●● = 

c 15 +  = 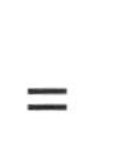

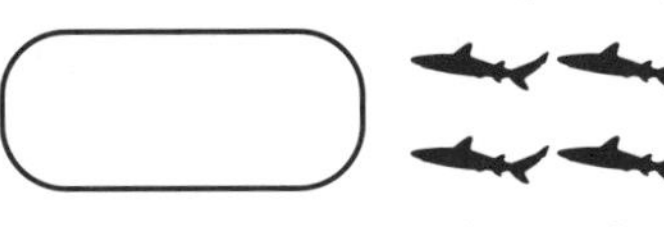

d 6 + ●●●● = 

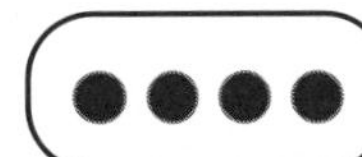

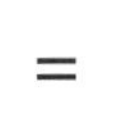

11:1 🦆🦆🦆🦆🦆 + 🦆🦆🦆🦆 = ☐

❶ Draw a tail on the mouse that is longer than 5 blocks and shorter than 8 blocks.

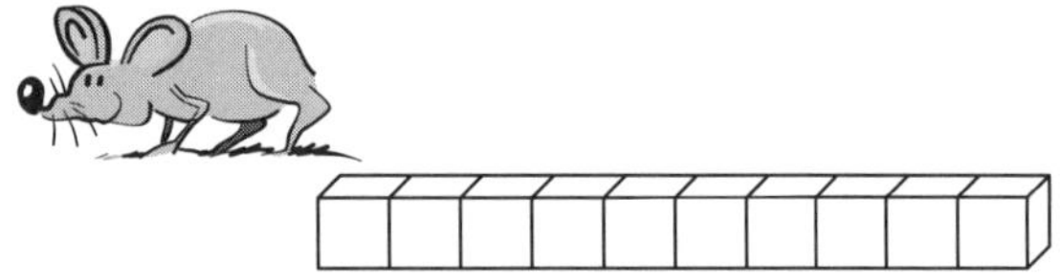

❷ Count on to find:

4 + 3 = ____ 6 + 5 = ____

5 + 2 = ____ 7 + 3 = ____

❸ Show these times.

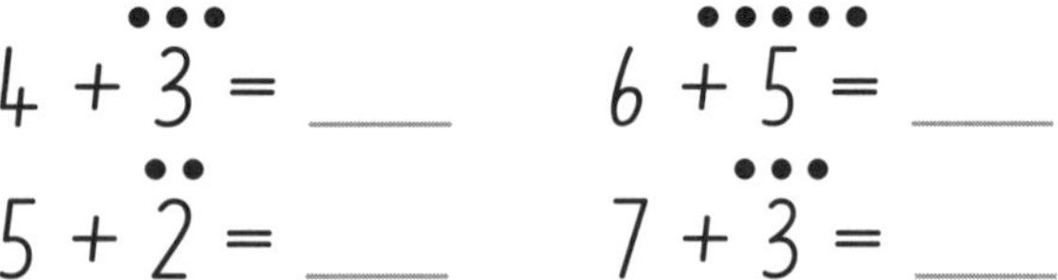

a a quarter to 3 b a quarter past 12

❹ Write two ways you can say this time.

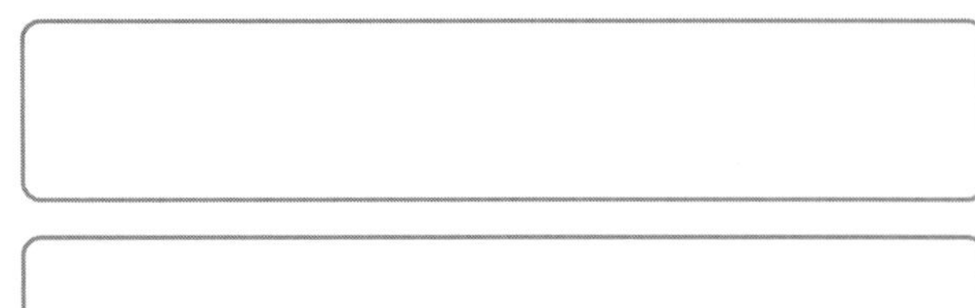

❺ Count on to find:

7 + 2 = ____ 9 + 3 = ____

8 + 4 = ____ 5 + 3 = ____

❻ Fill in the numbers on this clock face.

Show half past 7.

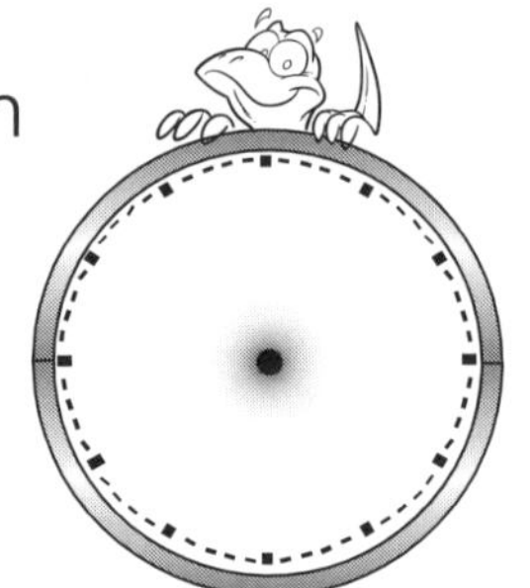

❼

11 + 4 = ______

❽ a

and

10 + 10 = ______

b and

6 + 7 = ______

❾ ____ tens ____ ones = ______

 ISBN 978 0 6557 0881 0

11:2

10, 20, 30, 40, ______, ______, ______, ______, ______, ______

❶ Complete the numeral expander and write the whole number.

a 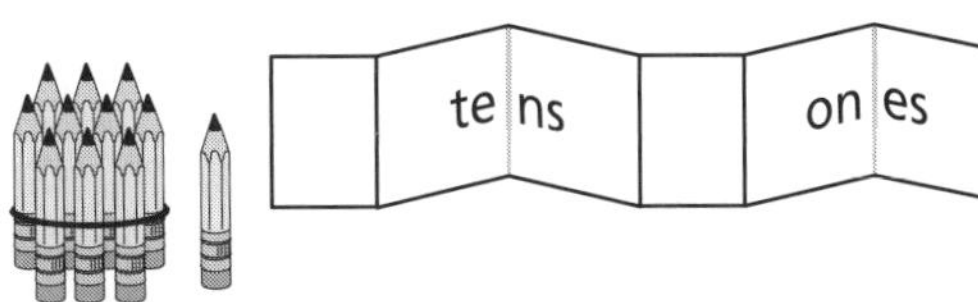

tens | ones

______

b 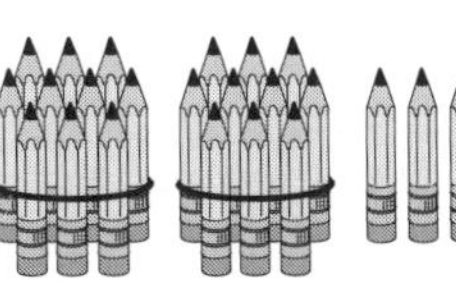

tens | ones

______

c 

tens | ones

______

d 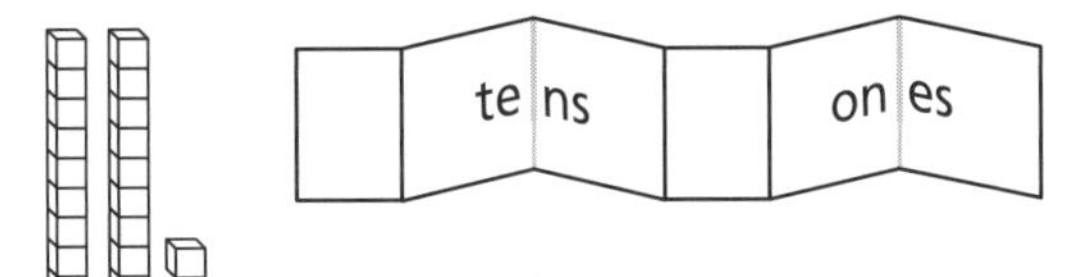

tens | ones

______

e 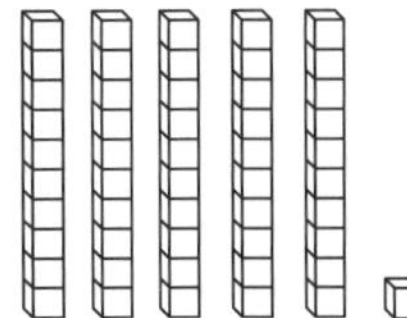
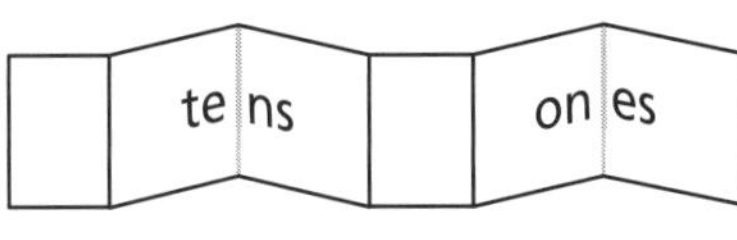

tens | ones

______

f 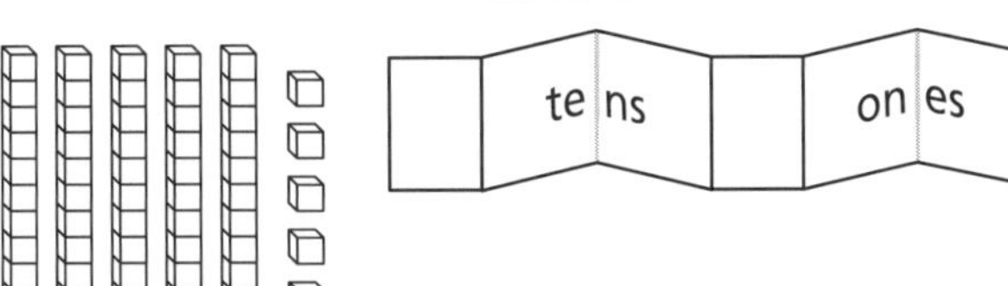

tens | ones

______

g 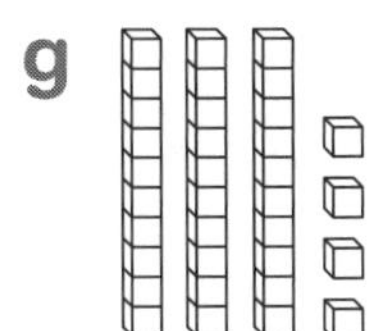
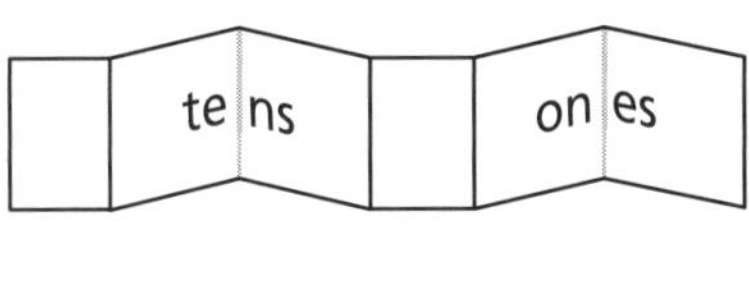

tens | ones

______

❷ a 20, 19, 18, ______, ______, ______, ______, ______, ______, ______, ______

b 6, 7, 8, ______, ______, ______, ______, ______, ______, ______, ______

11:3

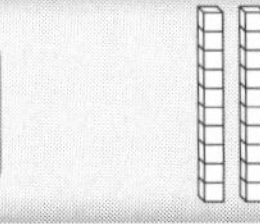

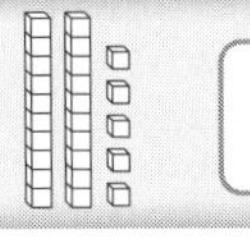
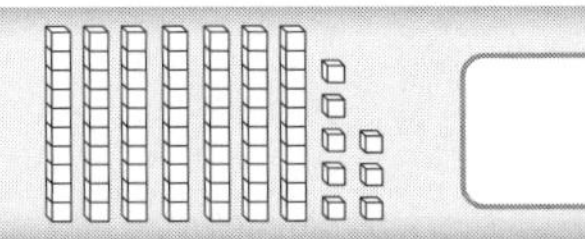

❶ a 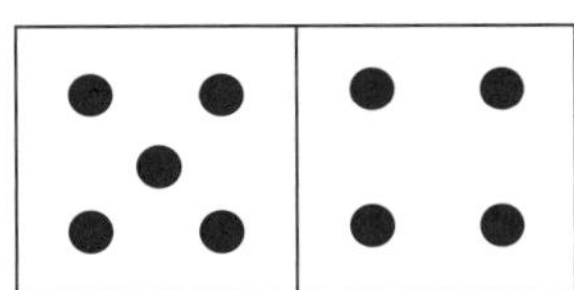

______ + ______ = ______

b 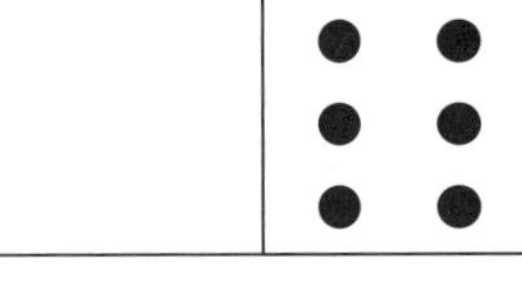

______ + ______ = ______

❷ Say the bigger number first and count on using the dots.

a 5 + 2 = ______ b 4 + 5 = ______

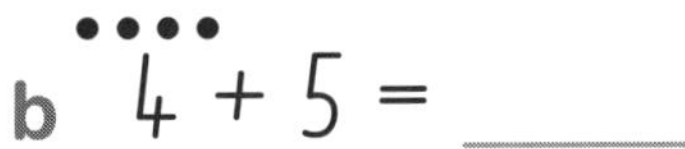

c 6 + 3 = ______ d 1 + 9 = ______

1 

7 + 5 = ____

2 

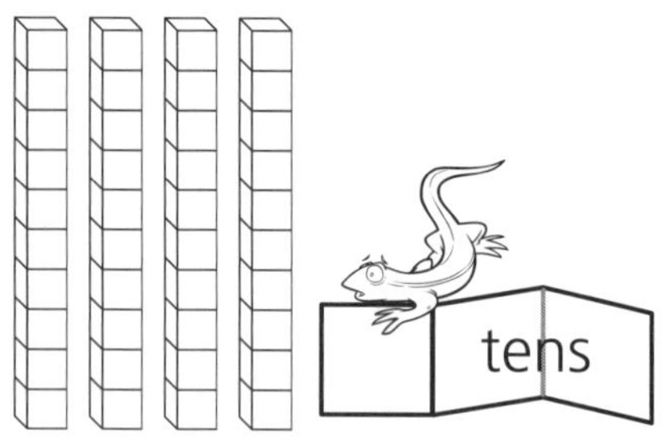

____

3 Write the missing ordinal numbers.

1st, ________, 3rd, 4th, ________

4 How many squares would be the same length as the rectangle? ________

5 

12 take away 5 equals ________.

Tick when done.

☐ Start at 1. Try to count to 100. My last number was ________.

6 Write the numerals in order, from 11 down to 7.

____, ____, ____, ____, ____

7 The number shown here is ________.

8 The number before:

70 ________ 81 ________

9 Circle the one that can hold the most.

10 Estimate how many cups would fill the carton.

________ cups

11 Draw a flag on the **left** flag pole.

 • *AUSTRALIAN SIGNPOST MATHS 1 MENTALS* • ISBN 978 0 6557 0881 0

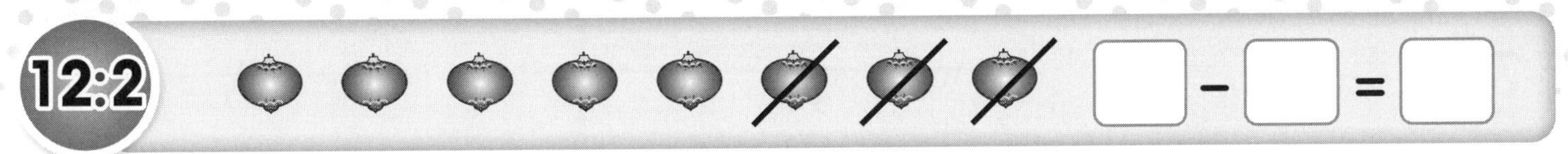

❶ Complete the numeral expander and write the whole number.

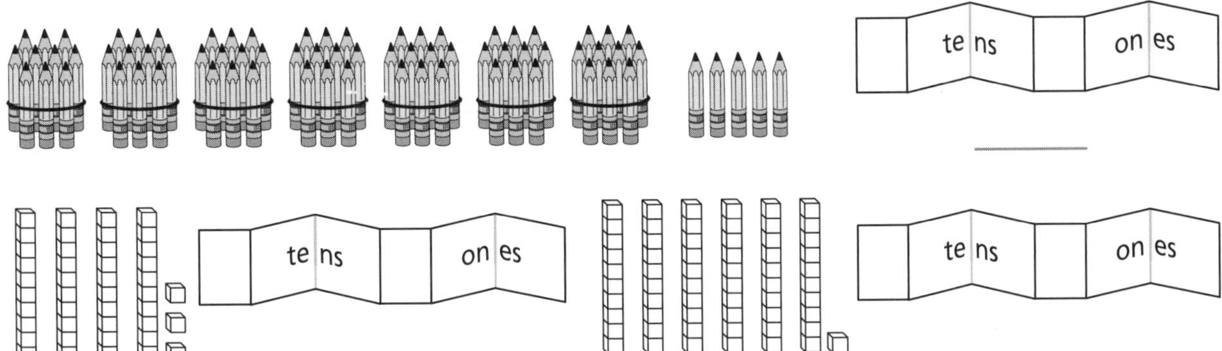

❷ Circle groups of ten. How many triangles? ______

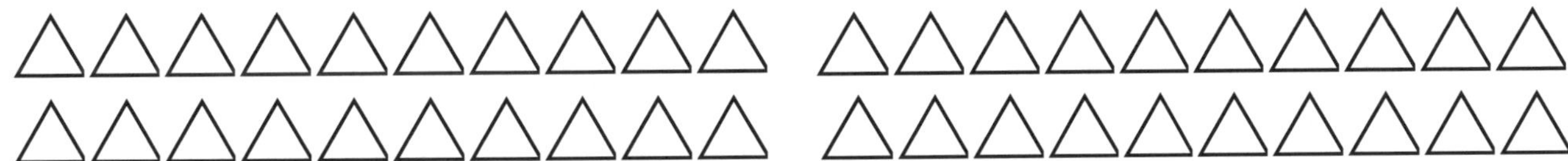

❸

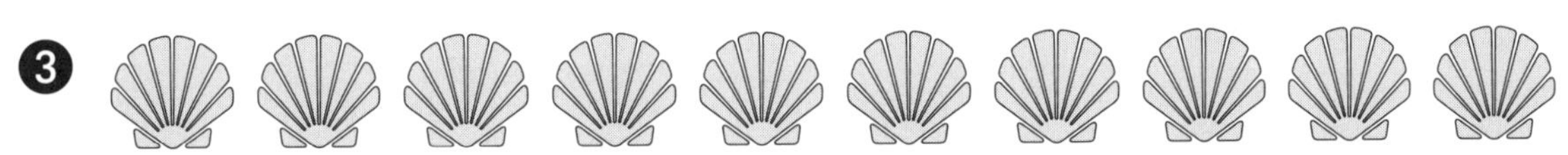

10 – 5 = ____ 10 – 4 = ____ 10 – 6 = ____ 10 – 3 = ____

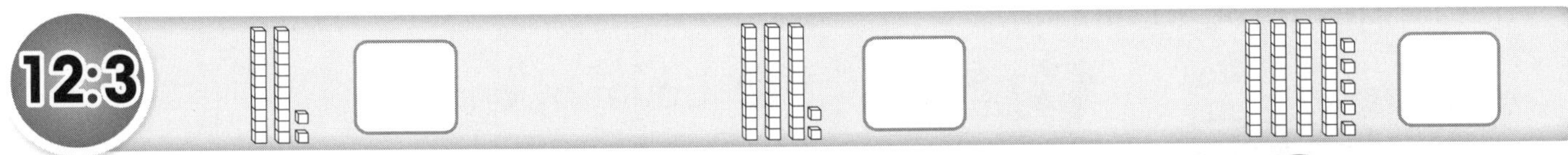

❶ Complete each number bond house.

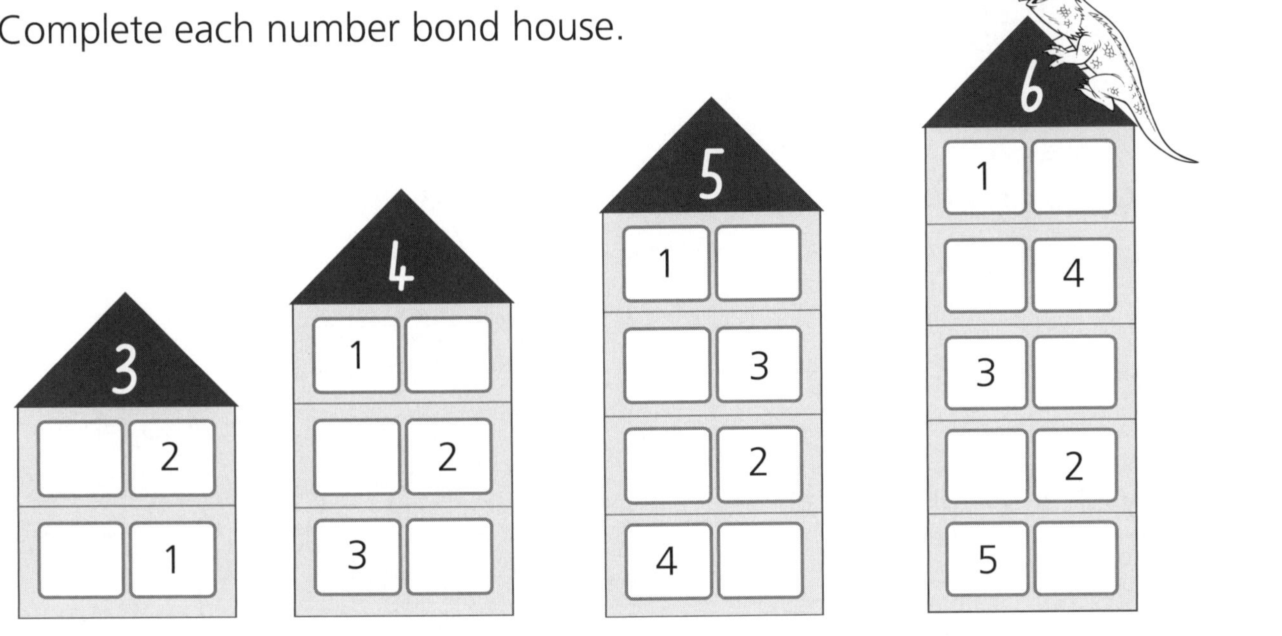

13:1

1 2 3 4 5 6 7 8 9 10

1 Use the number line above to help you answer these:

3 + 2 = ______ 6 + 4 = ______

5 plus 3 makes ______.

2 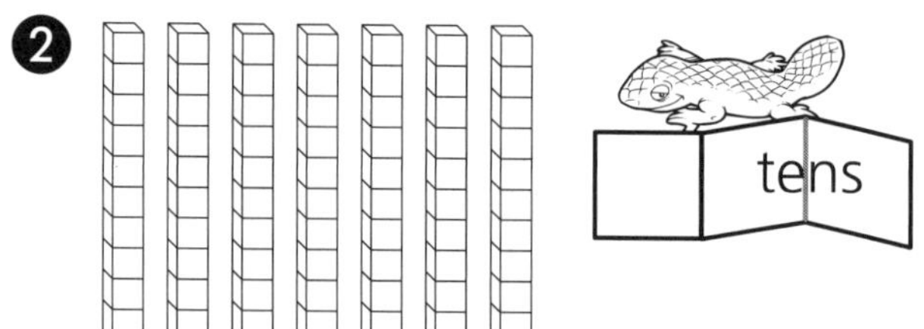

______

3 Write the number sentence.

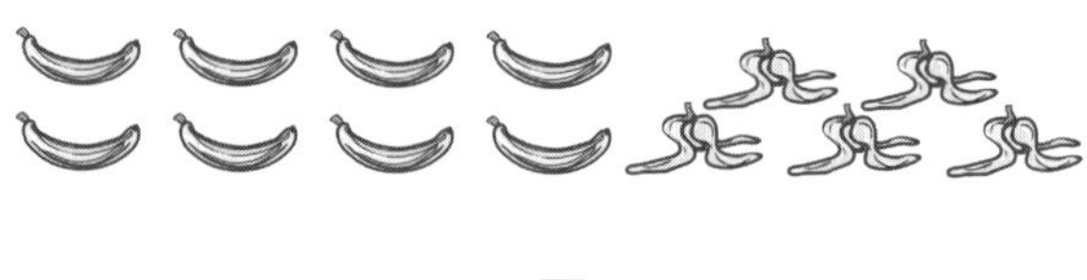

______ − ______ = ______

4 Tick the bucket that would take the longest time to fill.

5 Count on to find the total.

8 + 2 = ______ 13 + 2 = ______

15 + 1 = ______ 16 + 3 = ______

6 The day after Wednesday is

______.

7 Write the numeral for:

a four ______

b seven ______

c eleven ______

d eighteen ______

e eight ______

8 Write the number sentence.

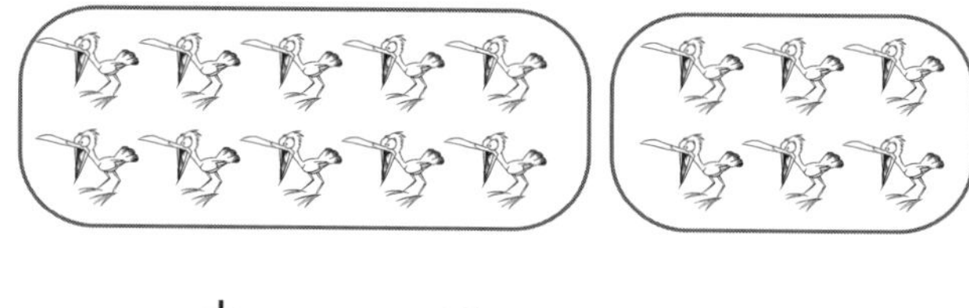

______ + ______ = ______

9 The number after 23. ______

The number before 27. ______

10 Count by ones.

26, 27, ______, ______, ______

11 20, 30, 40, ______, ______

80, 70, 60, ______, ______

Tick when done.

- [ ] Start at 10. Count by 10s to 100.
- [ ] Start at 100. Count back by 10s to 0.

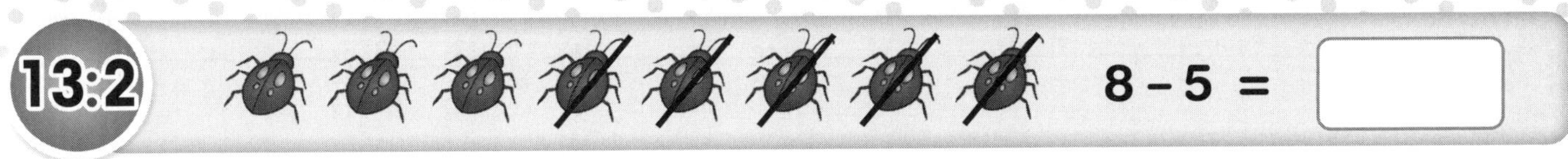

❶ Write the number shown. Each bundle is 10.

a  ______

b  ______

c  ______

d  ______

e ______

f 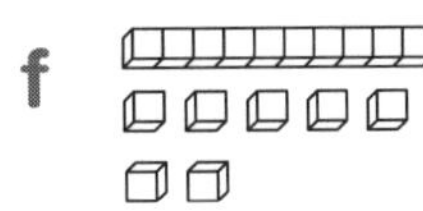 ______

❷ Draw a tree on the **left** of the car and a flower on the **right** of the car.

❸ Today is ______________. Yesterday was ______________.

Tomorrow will be ______________.

❶ There are 10 coins in each group. Some are covered.
Write how many coins have been covered by the hand.

a  ______

b  ______

c  ______

d 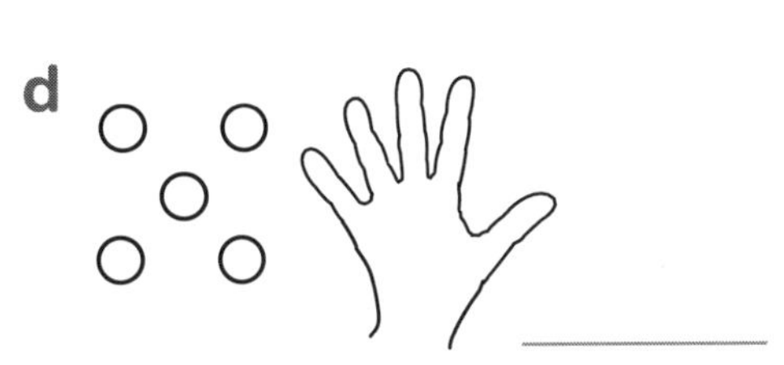 ______

14:1

0 1 2 3 4 5 6 7 8 9 10 11 12 13 14 15 16 17 18 19 20

1. Use the number line above to help you answer these:

   6 + 5 = ______ 7 + 4 = ______

   8 plus 4 makes ______.

   9 plus 5 makes ______.

2. Complete:

   ______ − ______ = ______

3. Match the names and numerals.

eighty-three	38
ninety-two	29
thirty-eight	83
twenty-nine	92

4. Count on to find how many altogether:

   11 + 2 = ____ 16 + 2 = ____

   17 + 1 = ____ 13 + 3 = ____

5. 19, 18, 17, ______, ______

   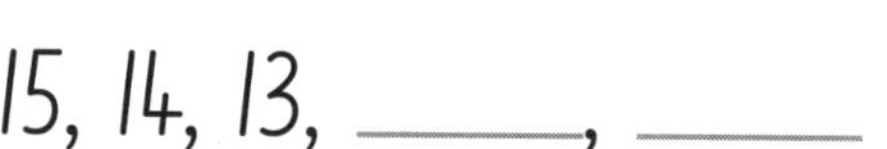

   15, 14, 13, ______, ______

6. Put these numbers in order.

43, 61, 58, 25

______, ______, ______, ______

7. Use the number line to find the nearest ten to:

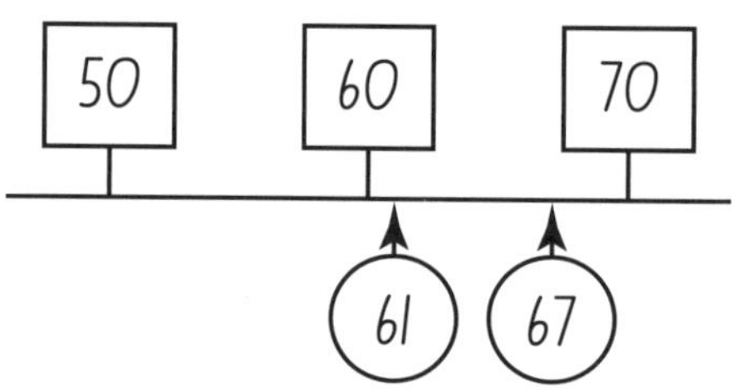

61 ______ 67 ______

8. A hexagon has ______ sides and ______ vertices.

9. What shapes are used to make this pattern?

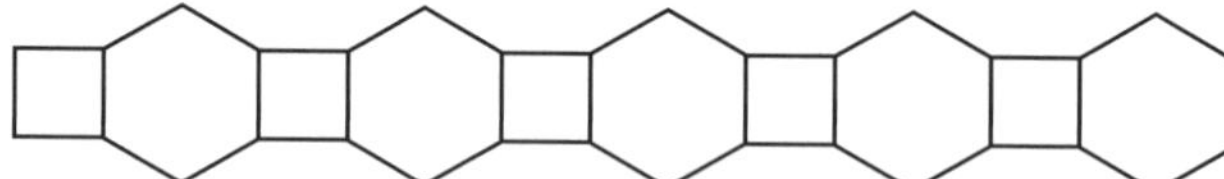

______ and ______

Tick when done. Count from:

☐	6 to 12	☐	13 to 8
☐	8 to 15	☐	16 to 10
☐	5 to 10	☐	14 to 9
☐	9 to 14	☐	18 to 12

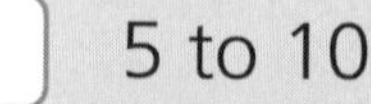
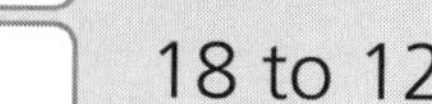

14:2

squares

❶ Fill in the missing numbers in the table.

1	2	3	4	5	6	7	8	9	10
11		13	14		16	17		19	
	22	23		25	26	27	28	29	30
31	32	33	34	35		37			40
	42		44	45	46		48	49	50

14:3 True or false? 2 + 6 = 6 + 2

❶ Complete each number bond house. Each row adds to make the number at the top of the house.

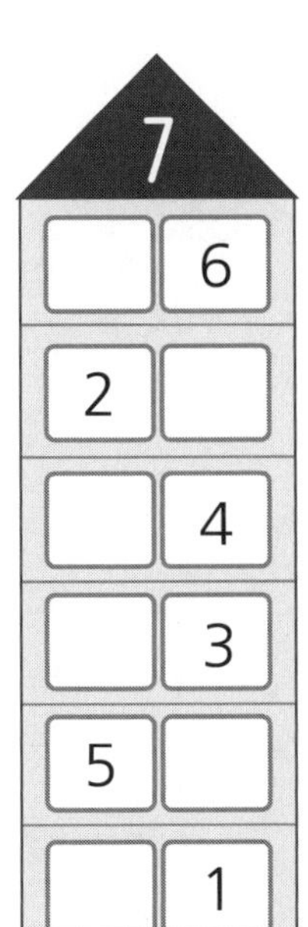

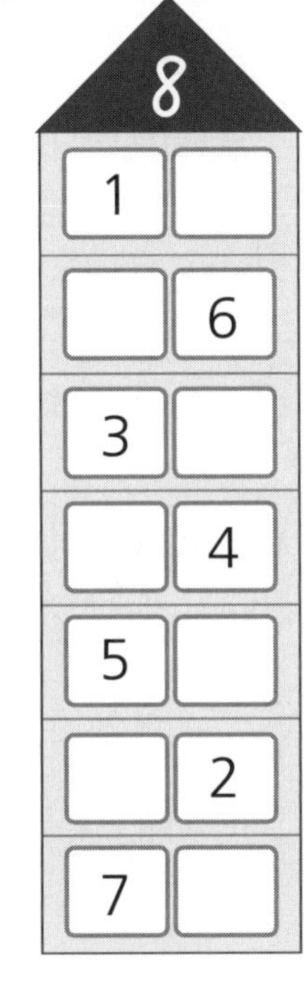

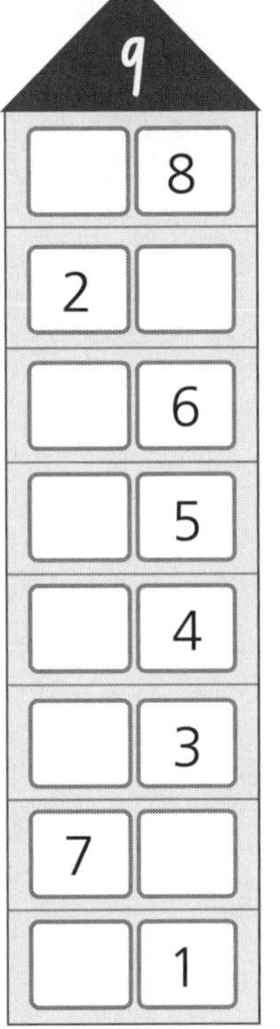

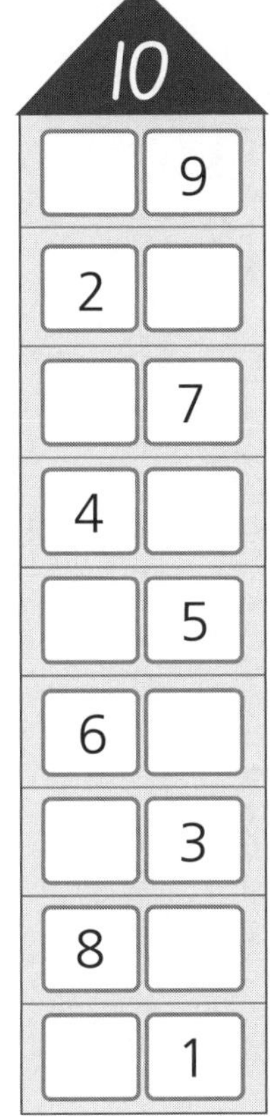

15:1

    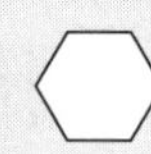

1 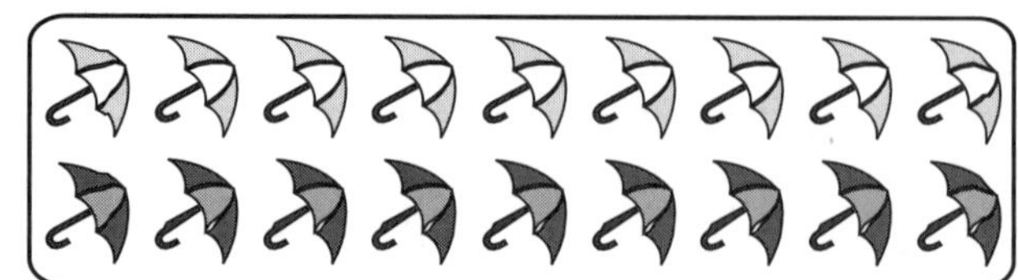

18 take away 9 equals ______.

2 Write the numeral:

thirty-seven ______

ninety-eight ______

one hundred and twelve ______

one hundred and eighteen ______

3 Use the number line to find the nearest ten to:

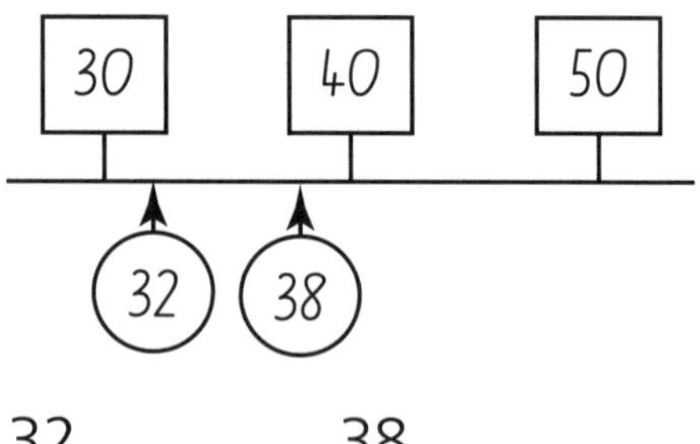

32 ______ 38 ______

4 What is one more than:

45 ______ 67 ______

5 20, 19, 18, ______, ______

8, 9, 10, ______, ______

6 Circle the lighter object.

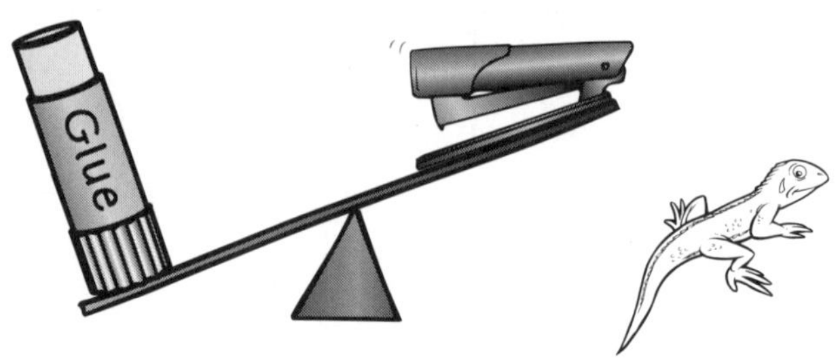

7

a How many koalas? ______

b How many kangaroos? ______

c How many platypuses? ______

d Which column has the least animals? ______

e Which column has the most? ______

 • *AUSTRALIAN SIGNPOST MATHS 1 MENTALS* • ISBN 978 0 6557 0881 0

15:2

❶ How many:

a squares? ______

b rectangles? ______

c triangles? ______

d circles? ______

e hexagons? ______

❷ Colour the design using the same colour for each shape.

❸ Draw a lighter thing on each pan balance scale.

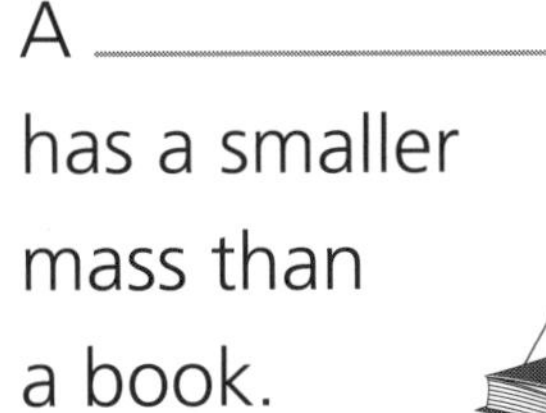

A ______ has a smaller mass than a book.

A ______ has a smaller mass than a bottle.

15:3

❶ Where do you finish?

0 1 2 3 4 5 6 7 8 9 10 11

a Start at 9, count backwards 4 = ____

b Start at 9, count backwards 6 = ____

c 9 – 3 = ____ d 7 – 3 = ____ e 8 – 4 = ____ f 11 – 9 = ____

❷ Make a pattern by colouring these circles.

16:1

10 11 12 13 14 ___ ___ ___ ___ ___ 20

❶ Count back from:

a 7, ____, ____, ____

b 12, ____, ____, ____

c 18, ____, ____, ____

❷ Name the shapes used.

________ and ________

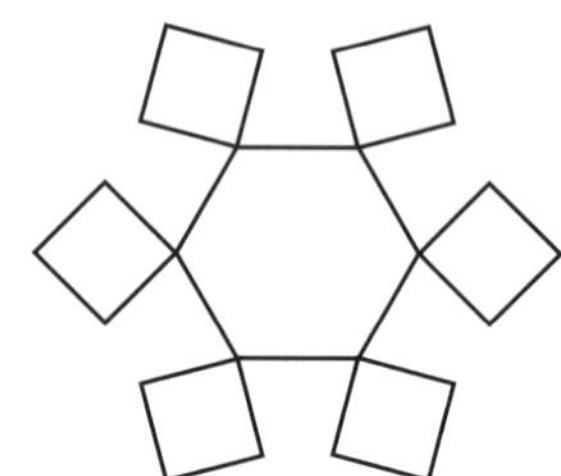

❸ Jack had 16 cars. He lost 5. How many does he have left?

____ − ____ = ____

❹ Count back to subtract 3.

a 16, ____, ____, ____

so 16 − 3 = ____

b 12, ____, ____, ____

so 12 − 3 = ____

❺ Write the name for:

a 29 ________

b 18 ________

❻ Complete the number line above. Use it to count back.

a 16 – 4 = ____

b 14 – 3 = ____

❼ Complete this pattern.

○ □ ○ □ ____

❽ On the scales, draw a picture of something that will be:

a lighter

b balanced

c heavier

❾ Draw an object that is about as long as your thumb.

16:2

1

Toys

Bikes	bike	bike	bike	bike	bike	bike
Scooters	scooter	scooter	scooter			
Skateboards	skateboard	skateboard	skateboard	skateboard	skateboard	
Skates	skate	skate	skate	skate		
	1	**2**	**3**	**4**	**5**	**6**

a How many skateboards? ________

b How many scooters? ________

c How many bikes? ________

d How many skates? ________

e How many more bikes than scooters? ________

f How many more skateboards than skates? ________

16:3

1 Complete each number bond house. Each row adds to make the number at the top of the house.

5	
	4
2	
3	
	1

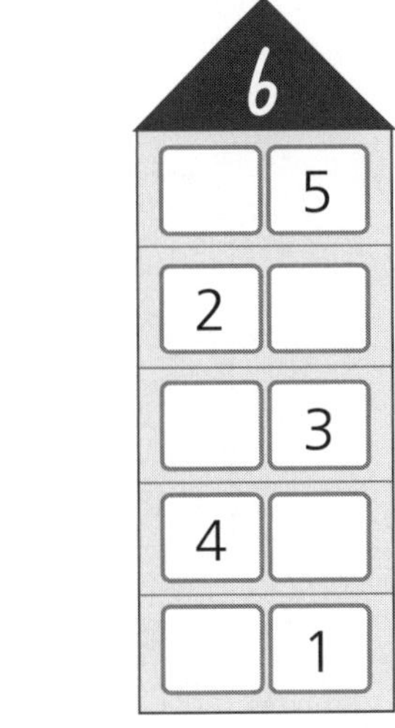

6	
	5
2	
	3
4	
	1

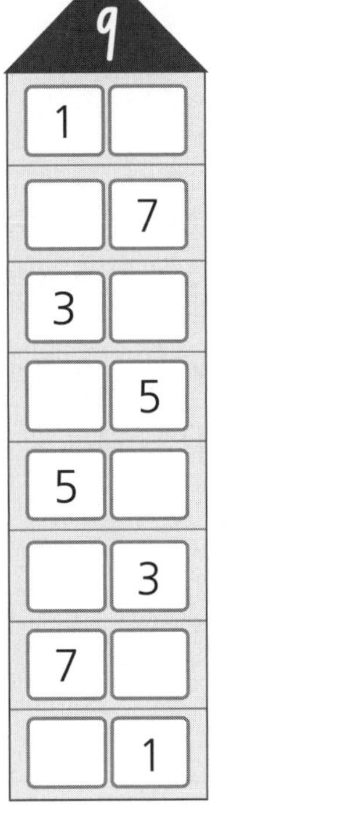

9	
1	
	7
3	
	5
5	
	3
7	
	1

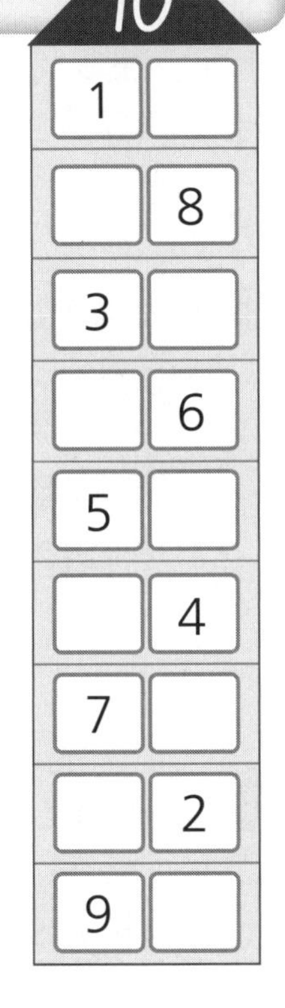

10	
1	
	8
3	
	6
5	
	4
7	
	2
9	

17:1

10 11 ___ ___ ___ ___ ___ 17 18 19 20

1 Count back from:

a 9, ____, ____, ____

b 14, ____, ____, ____

c 20, ____, ____, ____

2 Draw an object that is about as long as your foot.

3 Double 3 is ____.

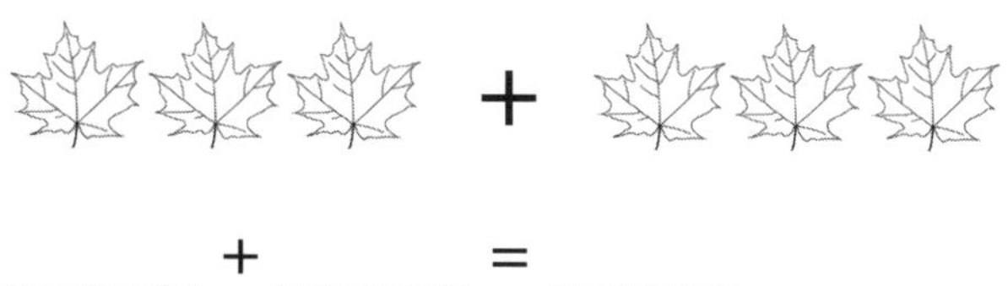

____ + ____ = ____

4 Lydia had 18 stickers. She used 3. How many does she have left?

Use the number line at the top of the page to help you.

____ − ____ = ____

5 This month is ____________.

Today is ____________.

6 Complete the number line above. Use it to help you find:

a 14 − 3 = ____

b 18 − 4 = ____

7 The summer months are

____________,

____________ and

____________.

8 Count back to subtract 3.

a 16, ____, ____, ____

so 16 − 3 = ____

b 12, ____, ____, ____

so 12 − 3 = ____

9

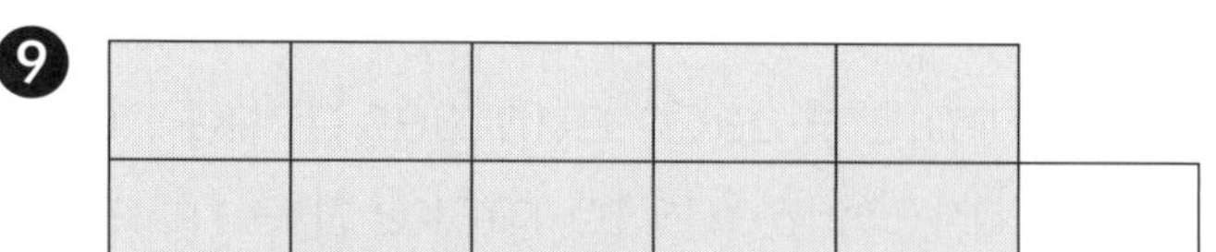

5 + 6 is double 5 plus ____.

5 + 5 + 1 = ____

Tick when done.

☐ Read these near doubles in your head.

1 + 2 = (1 + 1) + 1	2 + 3 = (2 + 2) + 1
= 2 + 1	= 4 + 1
= 3	= 5

Answers

ID card A

1 addition **2** subtraction
3 is equal to **4** number line
5 ordinal numbers **6** numeral expander
7 abacus **8** ones (place-value) block
9 tens (place-value) block
10 hundreds (place-value) block
11 dollar sign **12** cents sign **13** 5 cent coin **14** 10 cent coin
15 20 cent coin **16** 50 cent coin **17** $1 coin **18** $2 coin
19 $5 note **20** $10 note **21** $20 note **22** $50 note
23 $100 note **24** seasons **25** calendar **26** digital time
27 o'clock **28** half past **29** quarter past **30** quarter to

ID card B

1 circle **2** oval **3** triangle
4 square **5** rectangle **6** quadrilaterals
7 pentagon **8** hexagon **9** octagon **10** curved line
11 cube **12** sphere (ball-shaped object)
13 cylinder (can-shaped object)
14 cone (cone-shaped object) **15** prisms **16** left hand
17 right hand **18** reflection (or flip) **19** slide
20 line of symmetry **21** full **22** half full **23** empty
24 balance scales **25** picture graph **26** tally
27 number bonds **28** number bond house
29 odd number of socks **30** even number of socks

1:1

7 (tomatoes)

1 12 (leaves) **2** 3

3 Monday

4 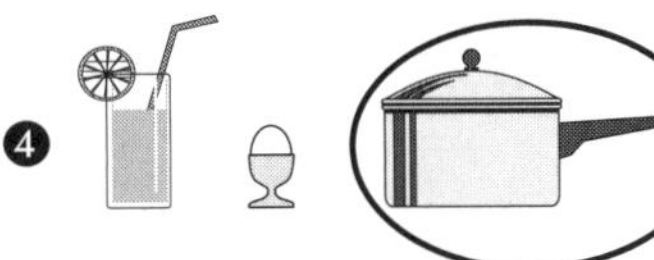

5 5 **6** 6, 7

7 8 take away 3 is equal to 5.

8 The pineapples will be circled.

9 

10 **a** 2, 3, 4, 5, 6, 7

b 10, 9, 8, 7, 6, 5

11 Answers will vary.

1:2

9 (beetles)

1 5 **2** 5 fish: 3 will be coloured red and 2 will be blue.

3 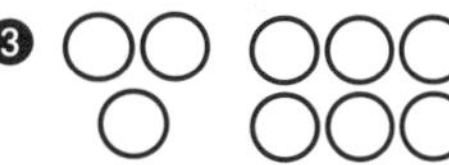 3 circles and 6 circles makes 9 circles.

1:3

1 The words will be traced. The correct number of shapes will be drawn to match each number.
8 (triangles), 11 (circles), 7 (rectangles).

2:1

6 (scooters)

1 The numerals and words will be traced.

2 3, 8, 10

3 circle

4  Two will not be crossed out. Answers will vary.

5 12, 11, 10, 9, 8, 7

6 **a** 2, 4, 6, 8 **b** 5, 6, 7, 8

7 5 **8** 16, 17, 18, 19, 20

9 Tuesday **10** 3 squares will be drawn.

2:2

10 (horses)

1 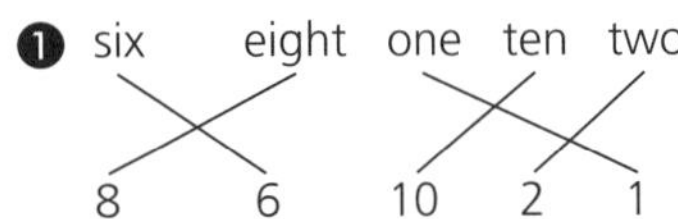

2 10 and 4 = 14, 10 and 7 = 17

3 10, 11, 12, 13

2:3

15 (strawberries)

1 The words will be traced. The correct number of shapes will be drawn to match each number.

5 (rectangles), 8 (squares), 6 (triangles)

3:1

15 (triangles)

1 7 **2**

3 3 milkshakes will be coloured pink and 2 yellow. 5 are coloured altogether.

4 **a** 10 **b** Scott **c** Christie **d** 3

5 11, 12, 13, 14, 15, 16, 17, 18, 19, 20

6 △ 8   7 3 and 2 makes 5. 5

8  

9 Possible answers are: 0 + 4, 1 and 3, 2 and 2, 3 and 1, 4 + 0.

3:2

12 (circles)

1 

2 0, 1, 2, 3, 4, 5, 6, 7, 8, 9, 10, 11, 12, 13

3 15, 16, 17, 18, 19, 20, 21, 22, 23

4 20, 19, 18, 17, 16, 15, 14, 13, 12

5 7

3:3

1 **a** 14 **b** 11 **c** 17 **d** 19 **e** 12 **f** 15

14 (squares), 12 (rectangles), 18 (triangles)

4:1

10 (frogs)

1 10 and 6 = 16

2 13, 20   3 17, 19

4 Answers will vary.

Possible answers are 0 + 7, 1 + 6, 2 + 5, 3 + 4, 4 + 3, 5 + 2, 6 + 1 and 7 + 0.

5 5   6 10 and 8 equals 18.

7 1 ball will be coloured blue and 3 yellow; 4 balls

8 7 o'clock   9 6 + 2 = 8

10 **a** 4 **b** 6 **c** 12

4:2

5 (fish)

1 Answers will vary.   2 6, 9, 16, 19

3    

4 8, 11, 13, 16

4:3

4 (goats)

1 3, 3; 4, 4, 4; 5, 5, 5, 5

9 (frogs), 19 (frogs)

5:1

10 (hot-air balloons)

1 18, 15   2 9 o'clock, 4 o'clock

3 14, 15, 16, 17, 18

4 Possible answers are: 0 + 9, 1 + 8, 2 + 7, 3 + 6, 4 + 5, 5 + 4, 6 + 3, 7 + 2, 8 + 1, 9 + 0.

5 **a** 1, 5, 7, 9 **b** 2, 3, 6, 8

6 17, 16, 15, 14, 13   7 12, 13, 15

8 The missing numbers are in the shaded boxes.

9 Estimates will vary. Count = 17

10 

5:2

10 (boats)

1

1	2	3	4	5	6	7	8	9	10
11	12	13	14	15	16	17	18	19	20

2 10, 11, 12, 13

3

9	6	5	3	1	8	2	4
1	4	5	7	9	2	8	6

5:3

7 o'clock, 5 o'clock, 9 o'clock, 4 o'clock, 10 o'clock, 6 o'clock, 8 o'clock, 12 o'clock, 11 o'clock

1 6, 6, 6, 6, 6; 7, 7, 7, 7, 7, 7; 8, 8, 8, 8, 8, 8, 8

6:1

5 + 1 = 6

1 12, 11, 10, 9, 8, 7, 6, 5

2

6	9	4	5
4	1	6	5

❸

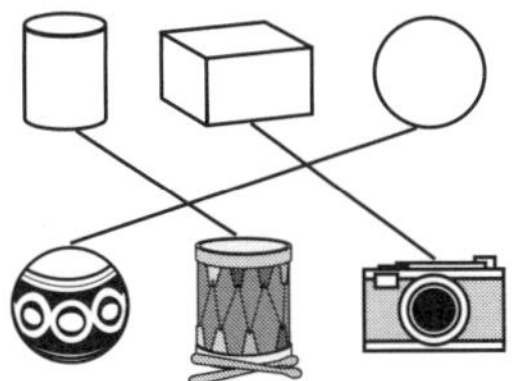

❹ The woman is to the <u>right</u> of the man, <u>behind</u> the trolley.

❺ 9, 8, 7, 8

❻

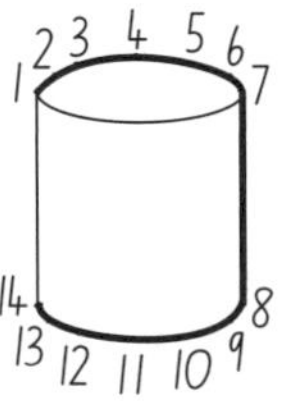

❼ 10 and <u>3</u> makes <u>13</u>. 10 + <u>3</u> = <u>13</u>

❽

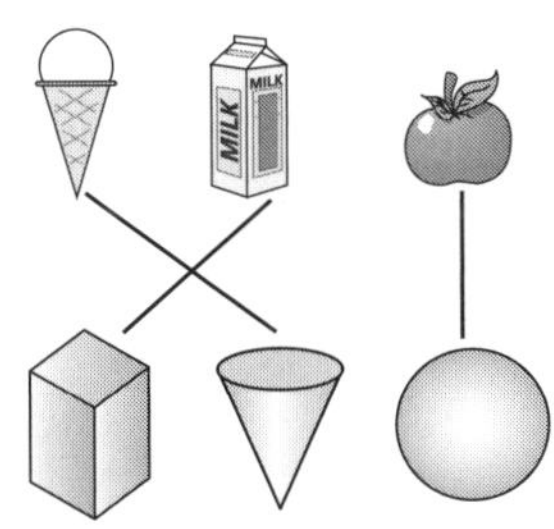

6:2

4 + <u>2</u> = 6

❶

❷ 5, 10, 9, 7
8, 10, 5, 10

❸ 11, 13, 15, 17, 19

6:3

3 + <u>3</u> = 6

❶ 1 + 9 = <u>10</u>

❷ 2 + 8 = <u>10</u>

❸ 3 + 7 = <u>10</u>

❹ 4 + 6 = <u>10</u>

16 (giraffes), 13 (dragonflies), 14 (penguins)

7:1

❶ 5, 10, 11, 14

❷

5	4	9	7
5	6	1	3

❸ 10

❹ 3 ❺ 7 (paperclips)

❻

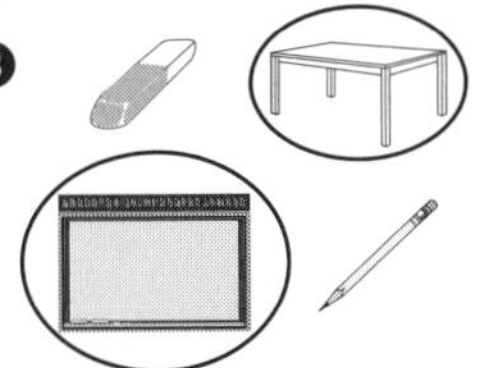

❼ 4 tens; 40

❽

7:2

7 (tens) = 70

❶ 10, 20, 30, <u>40</u>, <u>50</u>, <u>60</u>, <u>70</u>, <u>80</u>, <u>90</u>, <u>100</u>

90, 80, 70, <u>60</u>, <u>50</u>, <u>40</u>, <u>30</u>, <u>20</u>, <u>10</u>, <u>0</u>

❷ **a** 40, <u>50</u>, 60, <u>70</u> **b** <u>70</u>, 80, <u>90</u>

❸

4 + 3 — 7; 5 + 1 — 6; 2 + 3 — 5; 3 + 5 — 8

1 + 5 — 6; 3 + 2 — 5; 3 + 5 — 8; 3 + 4 — 7

❹

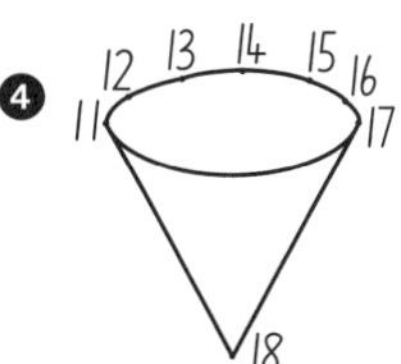

7:3

5 (stars)

❶

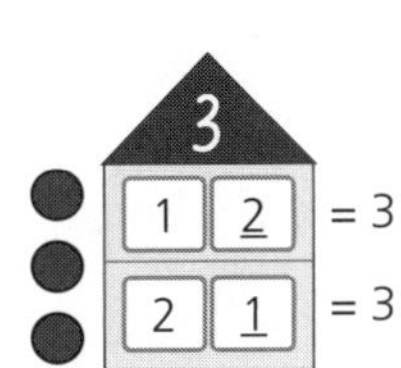

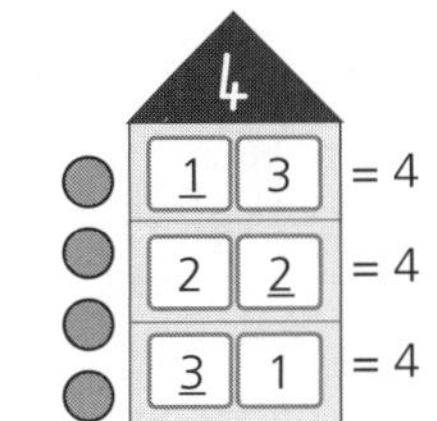

5

1 4 = 5

2 3 = 5

3 2 = 5

4 1 = 5

8:1

10, 20, 30, 40, 50, 60, 70, 80, 90, 100

1. thirty, sixty
2. The first pencil will be coloured. 3. 6
4.

4	5	6	7	8	9
14	15	16	17	18	19
24	25	26	27	28	29
34	35	36	37	38	39
44	45	46	47	48	49
54	55	56	57	58	59

5. 3
6. 10, 10, 10, 7, 8, 10, 10, 6 7. 6
8. a 23 b 51 c 82 d 69 9. 37, 56, 73, 81

8:2

60 (cents)

1. 
2. 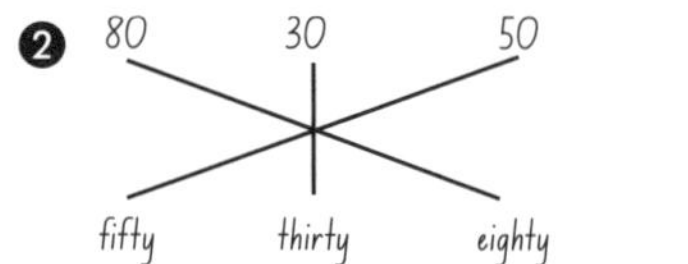

3. Estimates will vary. 50 is a good estimate. Count = 50

Groups of 10 = 5

8:3

4 (tens) = 40

1. 

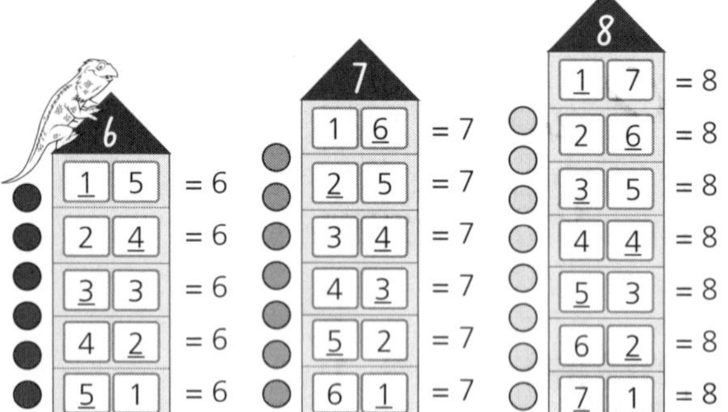

9:1

6 – 2 = 4 (ants)

1. 5 2. 7 3. 3 (o'clock), 8 (o'clock)
4. 10, 10
5. a 14, 15, 16, 17, 18

   b 22, 21, 20, 19, 18
6. a odd, 7 b even, 10
7. 13
8.

62	63	64	65	66	67
72	73	74	75	76	77

9. a  b

9:2

8 – 5 = 3 (balloons)

1. 1st, 2nd, 3rd, 4th, 5th
2.

60	61	62	63	64	65	66	67	68	69
70	71	72	73	74	75	76	77	78	79
80	81	82	83	84	85	86	87	88	89
90	91	92	93	94	95	96	97	98	99

3. 90, 80, 70, 60, 50, 40, 30, 20, 10, 0

9:3

10 + 4 = 14 (toy horses)

1. a 10, 10, 10, 10, 10, 10, 10, 10

   b 8, 8, 8, 8, 8, 8, 8, 8

   35 shells

10:1

11 (ants)

1. 6 + 4 = 10
2. 5 trees altogether
   take away 2 is equal to 3.
3. a even, 8 b odd, 7
4. quarter to 8, 7 forty-five or forty-five past 7; quarter to 11, 10 forty-five or forty-five past 10
5. 16 6. 8, 8, 6, 10
7. 70 8. half past 11, half past 5
9.  10. 

10:2

4 + 5 = 9

1. 10 and 2 = 12, 10 + 6 = 16

 ISBN 978 0 6557 0881 0

❷    

❸ 10 ,20, 30, 40, 50, 60, 70, 80, 90, 100

90, 80, 70, 60, 50, 40, 30, 20, 10, 0

10:3

5 + 4 = 9

❶ **a** 7 **b** 15 **c** 16 **d** 10

12 (seals), 15 (sheep), 18 (sharks)

11:1

9 (ducks)

❶ A tail will be drawn on the mouse that is longer than 5 blocks but shorter than 8 blocks.

❷ 7, 11, 7, 10

❸ **a**  **b** 

❹ Answers will vary but could include quarter to 9, 8 forty-five or forty-five past 8.

❺ 9, 12, 12, 8

❻ 

❼ 15 ❽ **a** 20 **b** 13 ❾ 6 tens 5 ones = 65

11:2

10, 20, 30, 40, 50, 60, 70, 80, 90, 100

❶ **a** 1 ten 1 one = 11
b 2 tens 3 ones = 23
c 5 tens 9 ones = 59
d 2 tens 2 ones = 22
e 5 tens 1 one = 51
f 5 tens 5 ones = 55
g 3 tens 4 ones = 34

❷ **a** 20, 19, 18, 17, 16, 15, 14, 13, 12, 11, 10

b 6, 7, 8, 9, 10, 11, 12, 13, 14, 15, 16

11:3

22, 43, 25, 78

❶ **a** 5 + 4 = 9 **b** 0 + 6 = 6

❷ **a** 7 **b** 9 **c** 9 **d** 10

8 (flamingoes), 9 (horses), 14 (owls)

12:1

The bath holds the most water.

❶ 12 ❷ 4 tens; 40

❸ 1st, 2nd, 3rd, 4th, 5th ❹ 4

❺ 7 ❻ 11, 10, 9, 8, 7

❼ 19 ❽ 69, 80

❾  

❿ Answers will vary. 4 is a good estimate.

⓫

12:2

8 − 3 = 5

❶ 7 tens 5 ones = 75; 4 tens 3 ones = 43; 6 tens 1 one = 61

❷

40 triangles

❸ 5, 6, 4, 7

12:3

22, 32, 45

❶ 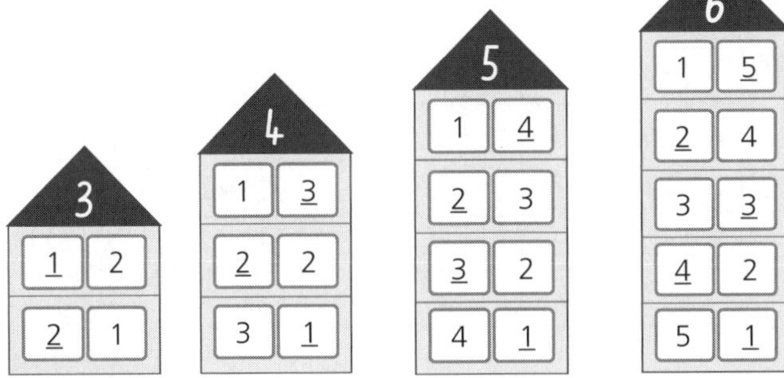

13:1

❶ 5, 10, 8 ❷ 7 tens = 70

❸ 13 − 5 = 8 ❹ The third bucket will be ticked.

❺ 10, 15, 16, 19 ❻ Thursday

❼ **a** 4 **b** 7 **c** 11 **d** 18 **e** 8 ❽ 10 + 6 = 16

❾ 24, 26 ❿ 26, 27, 28, 29, 30

⓫ 20, 30, 40, 50, 60

80, 70, 60, 50, 40

13:2

8 – 5 = 3

❶ **a** 12 **b** 13 **c** 15 **d** 20 **e** 19 **f** 17

❷  

❸ Answers will vary.

13:3

10 – 4 = 6

❶ **a** 4 **b** 7 **c** 6 **d** 5

31 birds

14:1

❶ 11, 11, 12, 14 ❷ 10 – 7 = 3

❸

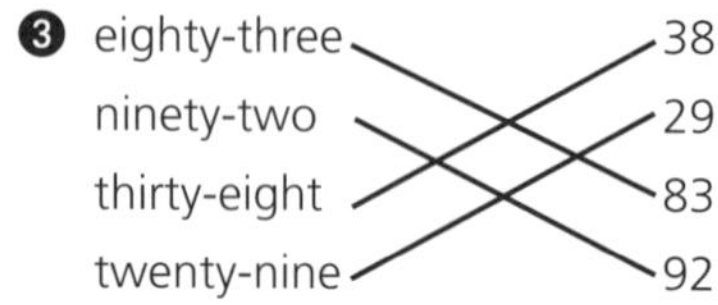

❹ 13, 18, 18, 16

❺ 19, 18, 17, 16, 15

15, 14, 13, 12, 11

❻ 25, 43, 58, 61 ❼ 60, 70

❽ 6, 6 ❾ squares and hexagons

14:2

18 (squares)

❶

1	2	3	4	5	6	7	8	9	10
11	12	13	14	15	16	17	18	19	20
21	22	23	24	25	26	27	28	29	30
31	32	33	34	35	36	37	38	39	40
41	42	43	44	45	46	47	48	49	50

14:3

true

❶

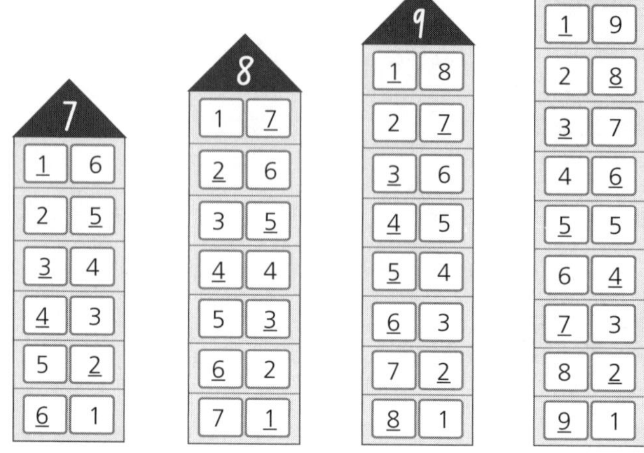

15:1

square, triangle, circle, rectangle, hexagon

❶ 9 ❷ 37, 98, 112, 118

❸ 30, 40 ❹ 46, 68

❺ 20, 19, 18, 17, 16

8, 9, 10, 11, 12

❻

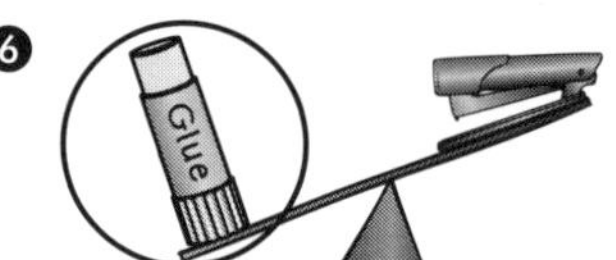

❼ **a** 5 **b** 3 **c** 1

d Platypuses **e** Koalas

15:2

46, 52

❶ **a** 1 **b** 8 **c** 4 **d** 4 **e** 4

❷ The shapes will be coloured so that similar shapes are the same colour.

❸ Answers will vary.

15:3

10 – 3 = 7

❶ **a** 5 **b** 3 **c** 6

d 4 **e** 4 **f** 2

❷ A pattern will be made by colouring the circles.

16:1

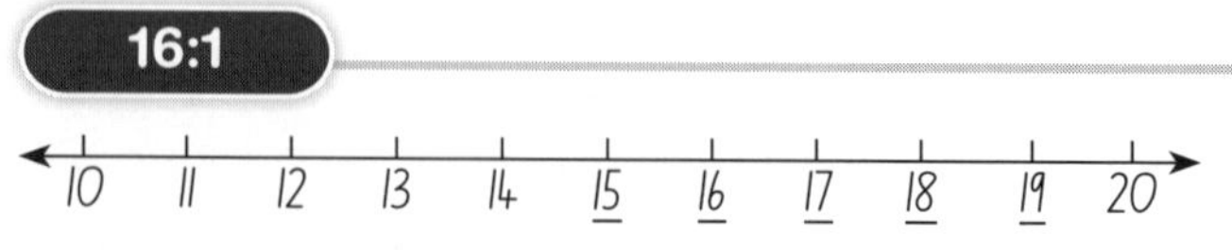

1 a 7, 6, 5, 4

b 12, 11, 10, 9

c 18, 17, 16, 15

2 squares and a hexagon

3 16 – 5 = 11

4 a 16, 15, 14, 13; 13

b 12, 11, 10, 9; 9

5 a twenty-nine b eighteen

6 a 12 b 11

7 

8 Answers will vary.

9 Answers will vary.

16:2

1, 2, 3, 4, 5, 6

1 a 5 b 3 c 6 d 4 e 3 f 1

16:3

square, triangle, hexagon, circle, rectangle, star, pentagon, octagon

1

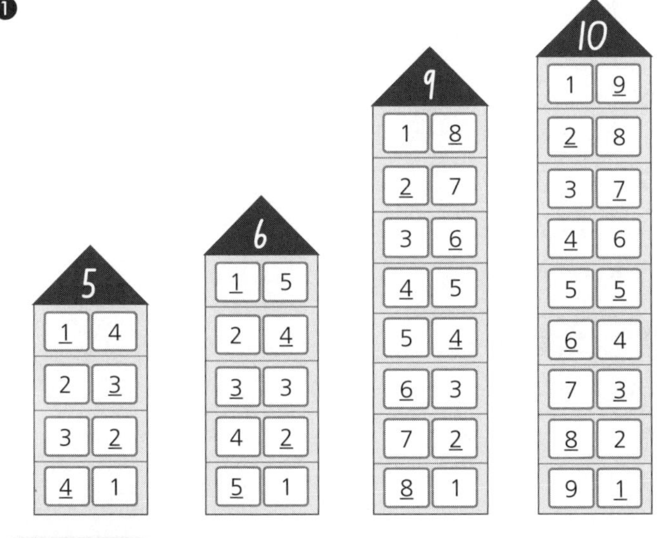

17:1

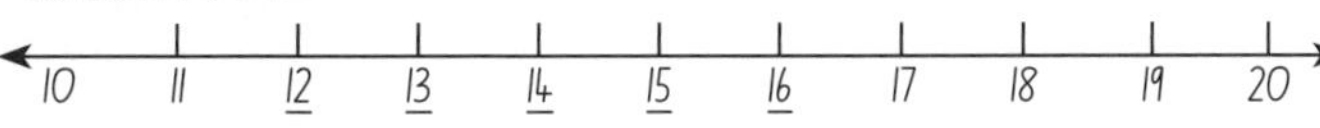

1 a 9, 8, 7, 6

b 14, 13, 12, 11

c 20, 19, 18, 17

2 Answers will vary. 3 Double 3 is 6. 3 + 3 = 6

4 18 – 3 = 15 5 Answers will vary.

6 a 11 b 14 7 December, January and February

8 a 16, 15, 14, 13; 13

b 12, 11, 10, 9; 9

9 1, 11

17:2

Double 2 = 4 (shells)

1 a 5 b 8 c 10
d 6 e 3 f 1
g Dogs h Horses

2 6, 18, 20

17:3

Double 10 = 20 (circles)

1 a 8; 4 + 4 = 8 b 10; 5 + 5 = 10

c 12; 6 + 6 = 12 d 16; 8 + 8 = 16

e 4; 2 + 2 = 4 f 14; 7 + 7 = 14

8 (deer), 12 (butterflies), 4 (octopuses), 12 (men), 16 (girls)

18:1

1 a 18, 17, 16, 15, 14

b 15, 14, 13, 12, 11

c 20, 19, 18, 17, 16

2 1; 15

3 June, July, August

4 10, 20, 30

5 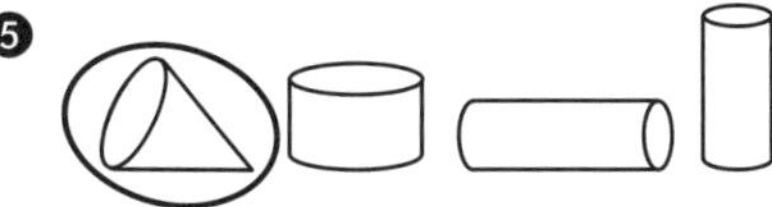

6 Answers will vary.

7 5 + 5 = 10; 10

8 6, 4, 2, 1, 1

9 7, 8, 6, 9, 8, 9

10 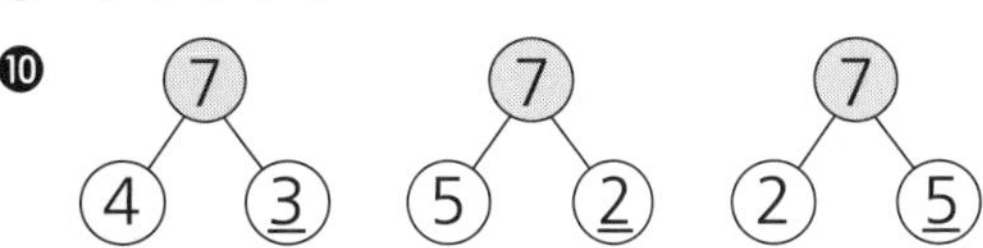

18:2

Double 3 = 6

1 a 30 b 44

2 1 January 2 February 3 March
4 April 5 May 6 June
7 July 8 August 9 September
10 October 11 November 12 December

18:3

2 + 3 = 5

❶

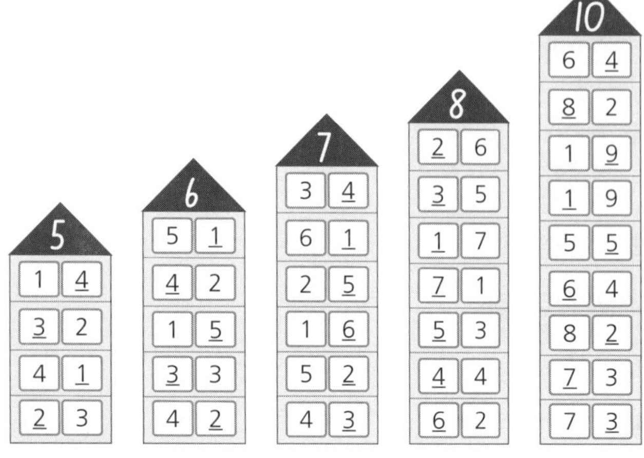

19:1

triangle, square, pentagon, hexagon, octagon

❶ 2; 2 ❷ 5, 5; 8, 8

❸

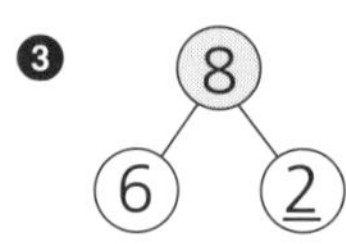
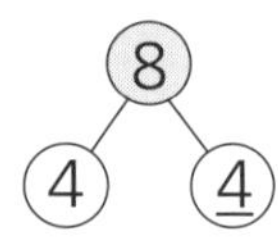
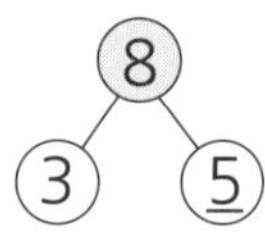

❹ 10, 8, 6, 9

❺

10	11	12
19	20	21

15	16	17
27	28	29

❻ quarter past 11, 11 fifteen or 15 past 11

❼ hexagon and rectangle

❽ 1, 2, 3, 4; The rule is add 1.

❾

19:2

7 – 4 = 3 (suns)

❶ hexagon, octagon

❷

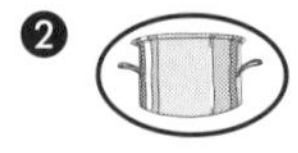

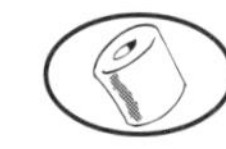

❸ 2, 4, 6, 8, 10; Add 2 is the rule.

19:3

Pattern: 3, 6, 9, 12

❶

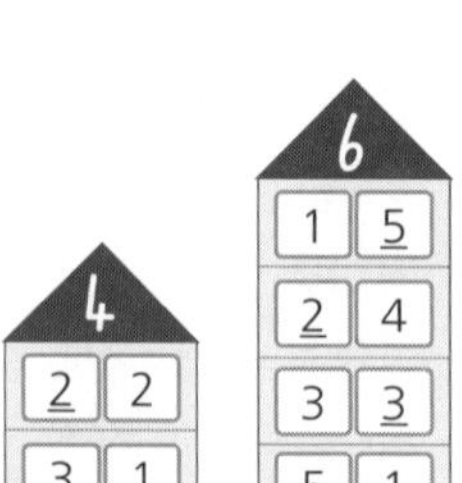

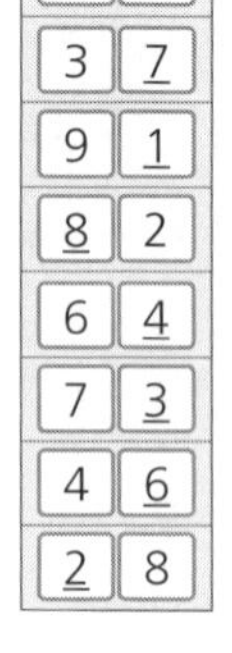

20:1

3 + 5 = 8

❶ 2; 10 – 8 = 2 ❷ 8, 8

❸ **a** 10 **b** 20 **c** 20 **d** 40

❹ 79 ❺ 21, 34

❻ **a** 79 **b** 40 **c** 83 **d** 108

❼ 89 will be circled. ❽ triangle, square

❾ A number bigger than 90 will be written.

❿ 5 tens 6 ones; 7 tens 2 ones ⓫ 10, 10, 11, 11

20:2

3 + 3 + 3 = 9

❶ 1 ten 2 ones, 12; 2 tens 3 ones, 23; 7 tens 5 ones, 75; 3 tens 2 ones, 32

❷ **a** 10, 20, 30, 40, 50, 60, 70, 80, 90, 100, 110, 120

b 74, 75, 76, 77, 78, 79, 80, 81, 82, 83, 84, 85

c 47, 48, 49, 50, 51, 52, 53, 54, 55, 56, 57, 58

20:3

4 + 6 = 10

❶ **a** 11 **b** 13 **c** 12

d 14 **e** 14 **f** 15

g 11 **h** 12 **i** 13

j 15 **k** 12 **l** 14

m 13 **n** 15 **o** 15

p 16 **q** 15 **r** 16

21:1

3 + 7 = 10

❶ 8 tens 2 ones, 4 tens 6 ones

❷ **a** twenty-nine **b** eighteen

❸ 6 + 4 = 10, 4

4 74

5 | 38 | 39 | 40 |

6 3

7 a 10 b 20 c 12 d 13

8 

  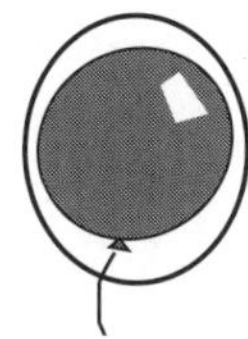

9 51 10 5 more balls will be drawn. 5 + 5 = 10, 10 – 5 = 5

11 33, 34

12 12, 11 13 10, 20, 30, 40, 50; 90, 80, 70, 60, 50

21:2

5 – 3 = 2

1 Each box can be ticked after the counting has been completed.

2 Students will count forwards and backwards by ones.

3 a 30 b 10 c 40 d 30 e 50

4 20, 31, 44, 63, 82

21:3

4 + 3 = 7

1 a 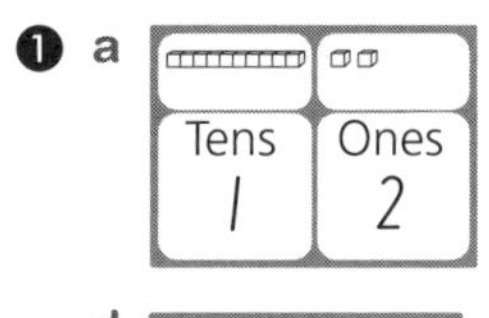

b 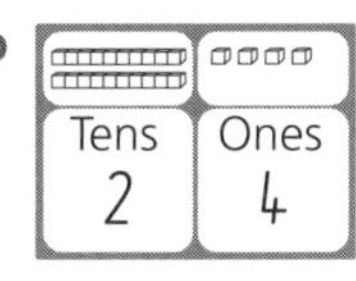

c 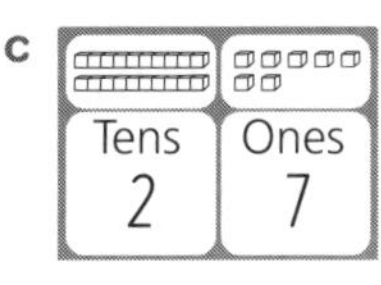

d 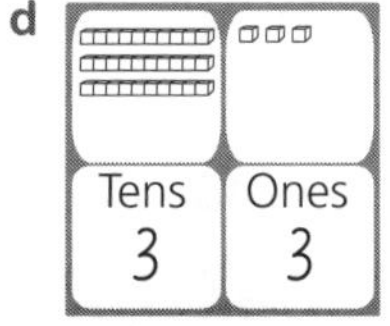

e 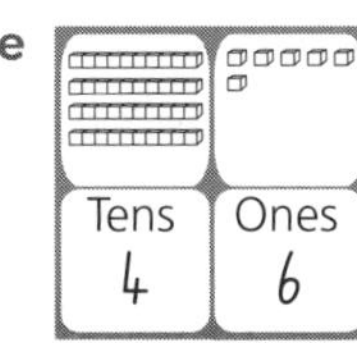

f 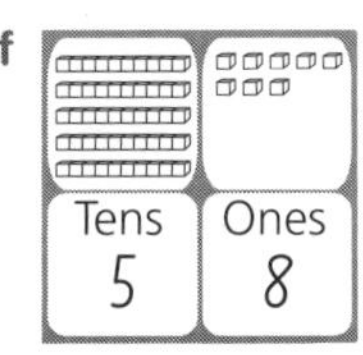

22:1

34, 67, 38

1 47 2 16, 94 3 94

4 4 groups of 3 = 12

3 + 3 + 3 + 3 = 12

5 59 will be circled.

6 7 stars will be drawn in the centre box. 3 groups of 8 = 24

7 3 more balls will be drawn. 6 + 3 = 9, 3

8 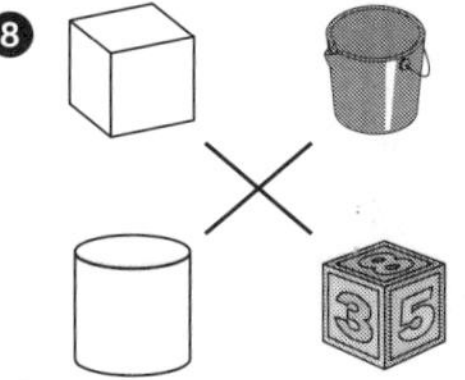

9 4 groups of 2 will be circled. 8, 4

10 4, 6, 9

22:2

3 + 3 + 3 = 9

1 a 4 groups of 3 flowers will be circled. 12, 12, 4

b 3 groups of 2 pencils will be circled. 6, 6, 3

2 8, 5, 3 3 3, 3

22:3

6 + 4 = 10

1 a 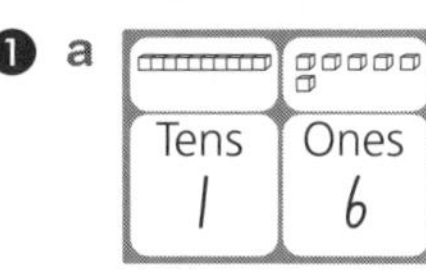

b

Tens	Ones
1	3

c 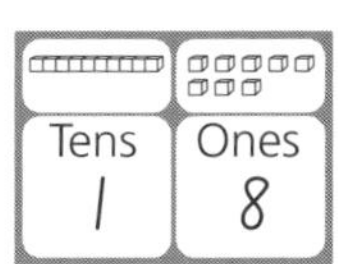

d

Tens	Ones
2	5

e

Tens	Ones
2	0

f

Tens	Ones
2	7

23:1

2, 4, 6, 8, 10, 12, 14, 16, 18

1 97 2 73, 91

3 a 63 will be circled. b 90 will be circled.

4 4 groups of 3 will be circled. 12, 4

5 a 5, 10, 15, 20, 25, 30 b 90, 80, 70, 60, 50, 40

6 4 tens 5 ones 7 3 groups of 4 cats = 12 cats altogether.

8 t-shirt: 2, stamp: 1, door: 3 9 8, 12, 18

10 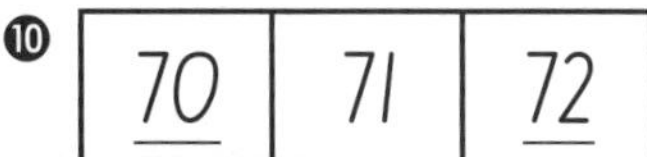

23:2

(4 groups of 3 = 12 crowns)

1 a 5, 10, 15, 20, 25, 30, 35, 40, 45

b 10, 20, 30, 40, 50, 60, 70, 80, 90

c 44, 45, 46, 47, 48, 49, 50, 51

d 67, 68, 69, 70, 71, 72, 73, 74

2 a 4 groups of 2 spoons will be circled. 8, 8, 4

b 2 groups of 4 guitars will be circled. 8, 8, 2

3 a September b 12 months

23:3

5, 10, 15, 20, 25, 30, 35, 40, 45

1. **a** 2, 4, 6, 8, 10 **b** 1, 3, 5, 7, 9
   c 10, 8, 6, 4, 2 **d** 5, 7, 9, 11, 13
   e 6, 8, 10, 12, 14 **f** 9, 7, 5, 3, 1
   g 14, 12, 10, 8, 6 **h** 13, 11, 9, 7, 5

24:1

10, 20, 30, 40, 50, 60, 70, 80, 90, 100

1. **a** 83, 84, 85, 86, 87, 88 **b** 64, 65, 66, 67, 68, 69
   c 10, 20, 30, 40, 50, 60 **d** 70, 60, 50, 40, 30, 20
   e 2, 4, 6, 8, 10, 12 **f** 50, 45, 40, 35, 30, 25
2. 8, 9
3. 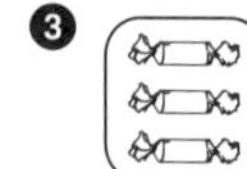 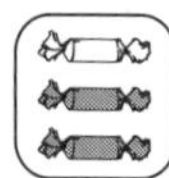 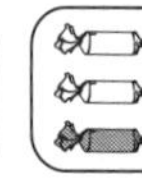 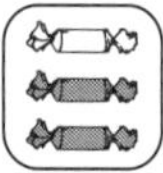

   3, 6, 9, 12 4 groups of 3 = 12
4. **a** 56, 57, 58, 59, 60 **b** 42, 43, 44, 45, 46
5. 
   5 groups of 5; 5, 10, 15, 20, 25; 25 (faces)
6. 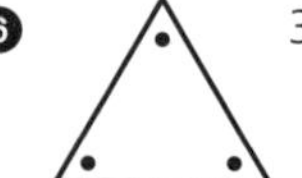 3  8
7. The words 'a tea towel' will be circled.
8. 3 groups of 2 circles will be drawn.

24:2

2 groups of 4 = 8 (soldiers)

1.    or  
2. **a** 5, 10, 15, 20, 25, 30, 35, 40, 45, 50, 55, 60
   b 0, 10, 20, 30, 40, 50, 60, 70, 80, 90, 100, 110
3. **a** 32 **b** 74 **c** 15 **d** 108 **e** 50 **f** 21
4. 5, 15, 9, 19, 9, 19, 9, 19

24:3

7 groups of 2 (circles)

4, 9, 6, 5, 8, 3, 10, 7

7, 9, 3, 6, 11, 10, 8, 5

25:1

23, 24, 25, 26; 57, 58, 59, 60

1. 20, 22, 24, 26, 28; 2, 4, 6, 8, 10, 12
2. 16, 16
3. 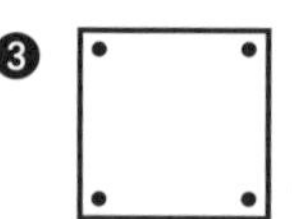 4 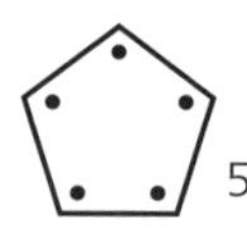 5
4. 4, 8, 6
5. 3, 6, 9, 12, 15, 18; add 3
6. **a** 6 **b** 10 **c** 10, 20, 30, 40, 50, 60 **d** 60
7. Answers will vary.
8. 8, 6

25:2

1. 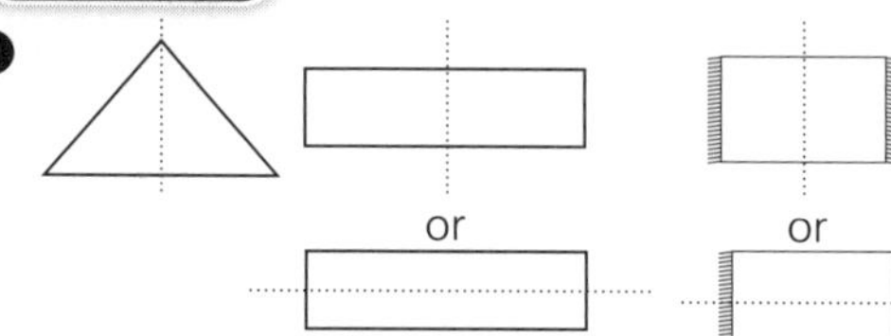

2. April, May, December
3. **a** 12 **b** May **c** 3rd **d** December
   e March will be circled. **f** July will be circled.

25:3

Pattern: 1, 2, 3, 4, 5; The rule is add 1.

1. 0, 2, 4, 5, 6, 7, 8, 9
   4, 7, 3, 6, 5, 1, 8, 0

26:1

5, 10, 15, 20, 25, 30, 35, 40, 45

1. 6, 12, 9
2. **a** hexagon, 6 (sides), 6 (vertices)
   b pentagon, 5 (sides), 5 (vertices)
3. 82
4. 63, 78
5. 10, 14, 10, 17
6. 17, 27, 43, 55
7. 8, 8
8. **a** 7, 9, 11, 13, 15, 17 **b** 12, 10, 8, 6, 4, 2
   c 40, 50, 60, 70, 80
9. **a** add 2 **b** subtract 2 **c** add 10
10. half past 10, 10 thirty or 30 minutes past 10

26:2

5, 15, 25, 35, 45, 55, 65, 75, 85, 95

1. January, February, March, April, May, June, July, August, September, October, November, December
2. Answers will vary.
3. 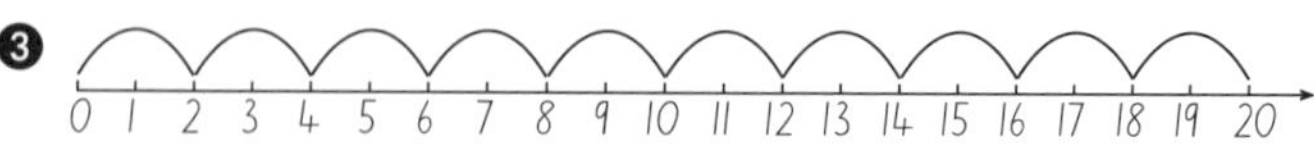

   a 0, 2, 4, 6, 8, 10, 12, 14, 16, 18, 20
   b 0, 2, 4, 6, 8, 0, 2, 4, 6, 8, 0 (or 0, 2, 4, 6, 8)

 • *AUSTRALIAN SIGNPOST MATHS 1 MENTALS* • ISBN 978 0 6557 0881 0

26:3

triangle, square, rectangle, pentagon, hexagon, octagon, circle

1 5, 9, 10, 9, 8, 9, 10, 8, 10, 11, 10, 8

2 Every 2nd bead will be coloured from the word 'Start'.

27:1

triangle, square, pentagon, hexagon, octagon

1 7, 7, 7 **2** 30, 29, 28, 27, 26;

3, 6, 9, 12, 15, 18; 30, 40, 50, 60, 70; 6, 16, 26, 36, 46;

10, 15, 20, 25, 30, 35; 16, 14, 12, 10, 8, 6

3 octagon, 8 (sides), 8 (vertices)

4 30 **5** 7 **6** 17, 17

7 hexagon

8 **a** 28 (days) **b** Tuesday **c** Monday **d** 4

9 11, 11, 15, 15

10 **a** 6 **b** 9 **c** 12 **d** 15

27:2

2, 4, 6, 8, 10, 12, 14, 16, 18, 20

1 30 days has September, April, June and November. All the rest have 31, except February alone, which has 28 days clear and 29 days each leap year.

2 Answers will vary.

27:3

4 groups of 5 = 20

1 4, 8, 6, 5, 9, 2, 3, 7, 1 **2** Every 5th bead will be coloured, starting from the bottom right.

28:1

3D objects: prism, cylinder, pyramid, sphere, prism, cone, cube

1 30 (days) **2** 7 (days)

3 3 counters go in each box. One share = 3 counters

4 10, 10 **5** **a** 8 **b** 12 **c** 16

6 **a** **b** The cube will be ticked.

7 C **8**

9 12, 12, 15, 11

28:2

1 **a** January, February, March, April, May, June, July, August, September, October, November, December

b 12 **c** 24 **d** 30 **e** 31 **f** 30

g August will be circled. **h** November will have a cross on it.

2 **a** 4 squares will be drawn in each box. One share = 4 squares

b 2 ovals will be drawn in each box. One share = 2 ovals

28:3

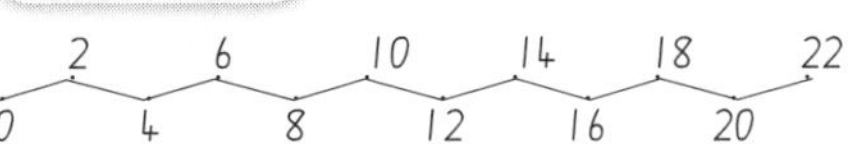

1

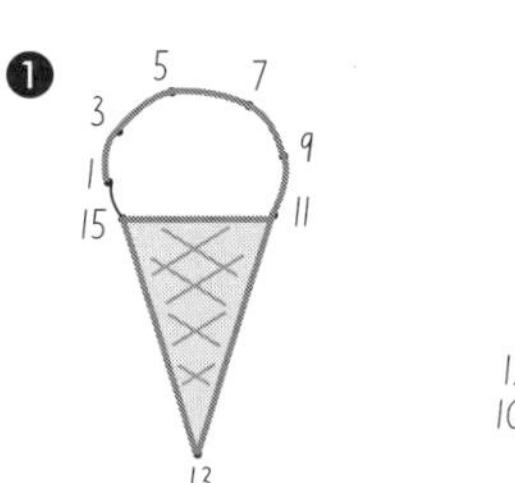

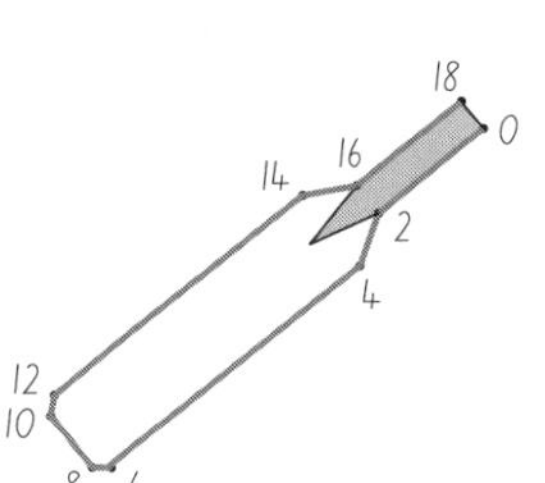

29:1

6 − 3 = 3

1 4 groups of 2 dolphins will be circled.

2 4 counters will be drawn in each box. One share = 4 counters

3

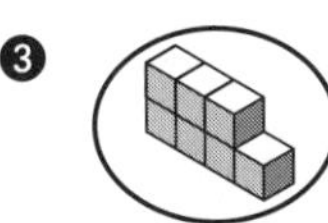

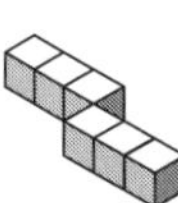

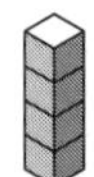

4 **a** 3 **b** 2 **5** no **6** Answers will vary. **7** 4

8 10, 10, 13, 17, 7, 9, 12, 14, 11, 13, 11, 11

29:2

1 **a** April, June, September, November will be circled.

b January, March, May, July, August, October, December will be underlined.

2 1st, 2nd, 3rd, 4th, 5th

3 **a** 3 **b** 6 **c** 4 **d** 1

29:3

3 groups of 2 = 6

1 4, 3, 5, 0, 5, 6, 7, 6, 3, 6, 6, 4, 3, 4, 7

30:1

One ball is heavier than 1 block.

One ball balances 2 blocks.

One ball is lighter than 3 blocks.

1 **a** 20 **b** 22

2 4 counters will be drawn in each box. One share = 4 counters

3 The 2nd rectangle will be coloured. **4** 10 (cubes)

5 10, 10 **6** 9, 4, 5 **7** 13, 7, 6

8 a 6 b 4 **9** yes **10** 10

30:2

3D objects: cube, sphere, cone, cylinder, cube, sphere, cone

(A pattern is forming.)

1 a 20 b 26 **2** a 11, 6, 5 b 12, 3, 9

3 37, 50, 64, 73, 96

30:3

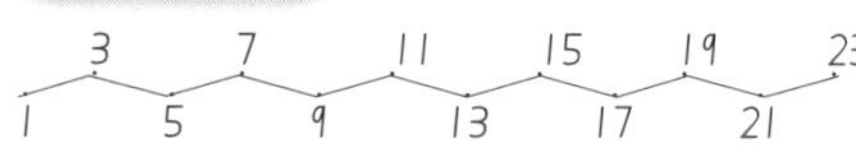

1 a 5, 10, 7, 3, 9, 12, 8, 11 b 8, 7, 13, 14, 11, 9, 12, 10

c 0, 3, 4, 5, 6, 7, 8, 9 d 4, 7, 1, 0, 8, 3, 6, 2

31:1

10, 15, 20, 25, 30, 35, 40, 45, 50

1 21, 23, 22, 27 **2** 3, 7, 10

3

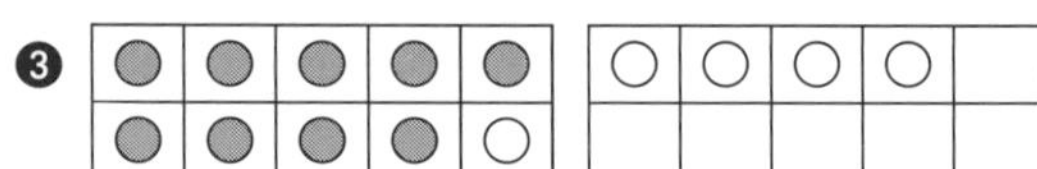

9 + 5 = 9 + 1 + 4

= 10 + 4 = 14

4 a 20 b 23

5

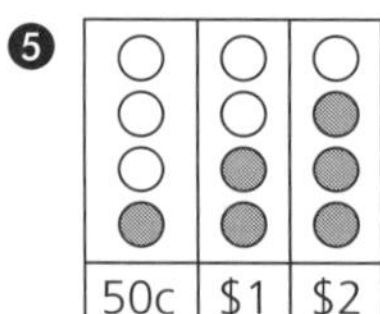

6 Answers will vary. **7** 4 (times) **8** 1st, 2nd, 3rd, 4th

9 93 **10** 61 will be circled.

31:2

1 a 31 b 33 c 32 d 32 e 32 f 33

2 28, 42, 79, 85, 94

3 a 36, 37, 38, 39, 40 b 22, 21, 20, 19, 18

c 10, 20, 30, 40, 50 d 2, 4, 6, 8, 10

31:3

7 + 8 = 15

1

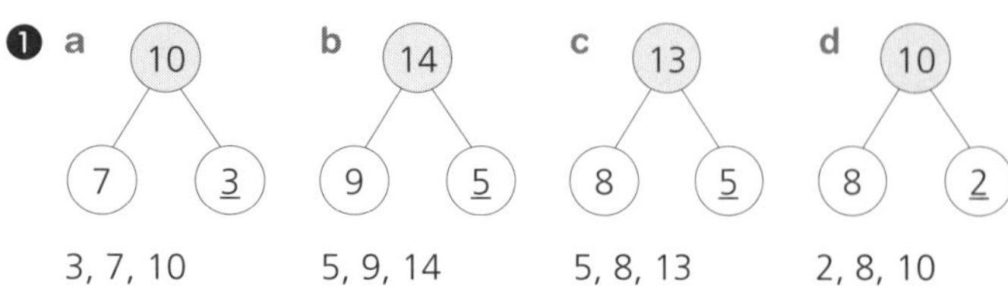

a 3, 7, 10 b 5, 9, 14 c 5, 8, 13 d 2, 8, 10

32:1

slide, reflection, slide

1 4, 4

2

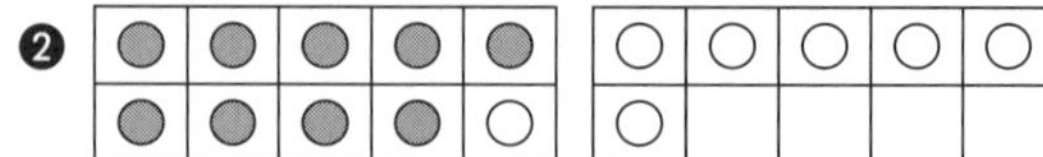

9 + 7 = 9 + 1 + 6

= 10 + 6 = 16

3 reflection **4** 39

5 A number smaller than 50 will be written.

6 ♣ (rocket) **7** 90 **8** 3, 16, 16, 7

9

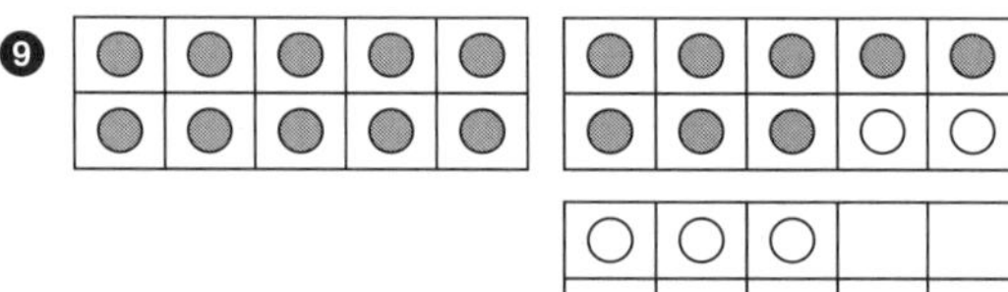

18 + 5 = 23

10 5 + 5 = 10 **11** 22, 23, 17, 19

32:2

1 a 28 b 28 c 26 d 27 e 28 f 28

2 a 4 b 7 c 4 d 25

32:3

5, 10, 15, 20, 25, 30, 35, 40, 45

1

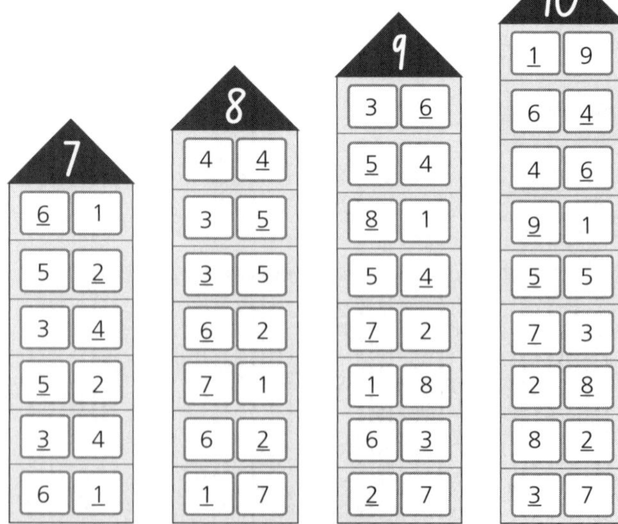

Multiple-choice questions

1 twenty-seven **2** 54 **3** 39 **4** 8 **5** 14

6 35 **7** triangle **8** hexagon **9** cube

10 drink bottle

 • *AUSTRALIAN SIGNPOST MATHS 1 MENTALS* • ISBN 978 0 6557 0881 0

17:2

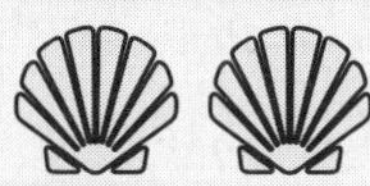

Double 2 = ☐

❶ **Animals**

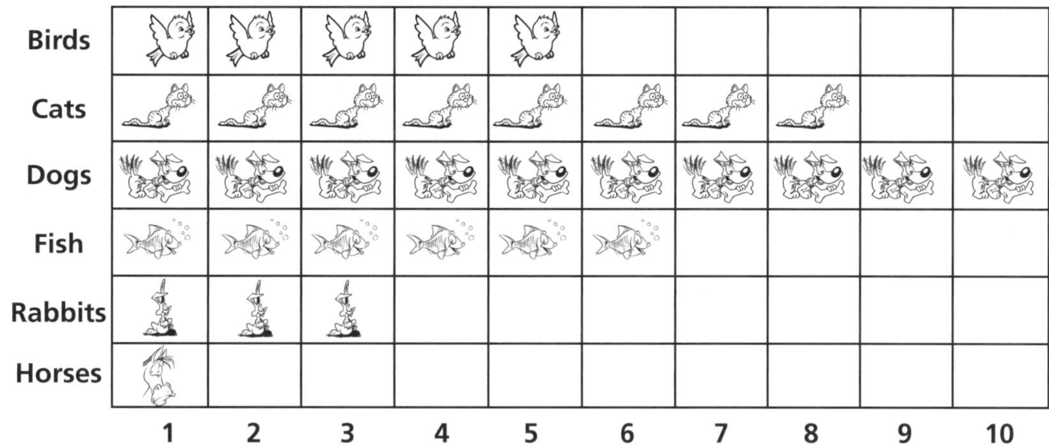

a How many birds? ________ **b** How many cats? ________

c How many dogs? ________ **d** How many fish? ________

e How many rabbits? ________ **f** How many horses? ________

g Which group has the most? ____________

h Which group has the least? ____________

❷ 3 + 3 = ______ 9 + 9 = ______ 10 + 10 = ______

17:3

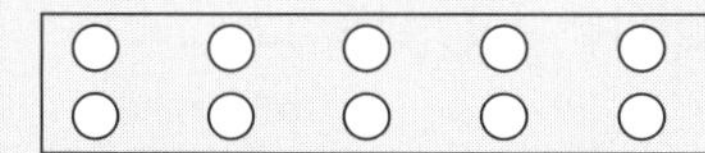

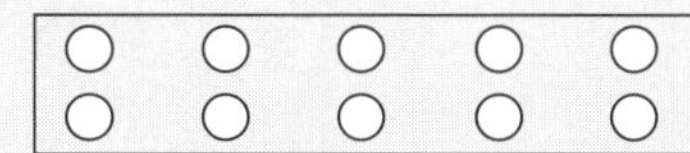

Double 10 = ☐

❶ **a** Double 4 = ______ **b** Double 5 = ______

______ + ______ = ______ ______ + ______ = ______

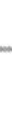

c Double 6 = ______ **d** Double 8 = ______

______ + ______ = ______ ______ + ______ = ______

e Double 2 = ______ **f** Double 7 = ______

______ + ______ = ______ ______ + ______ = ______

January, February, March, April, May, June, July, August, September, October, November, December

❶ Count backwards from:

a 18, ____, ____, ____, ____

b 15, ____, ____, ____, ____

c 20, ____, ____, ____, ____

❷ 7 + 8 is double 7 plus ____.

7 + 7 + 1 = ____

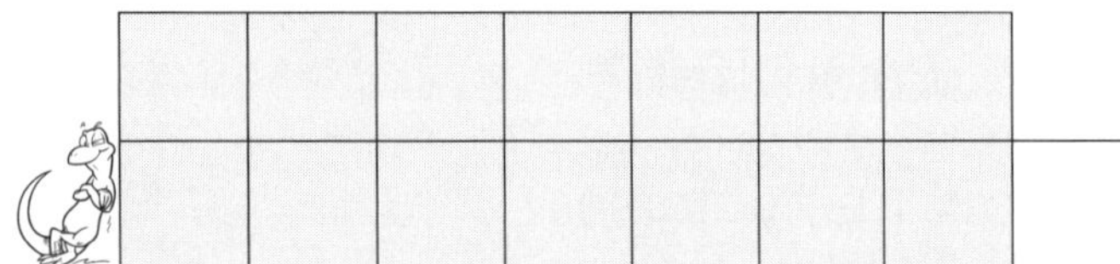

❸ The winter months are

____________________,

____________________ and

____________________.

❹ Write the number pattern.

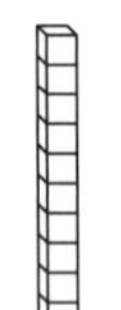
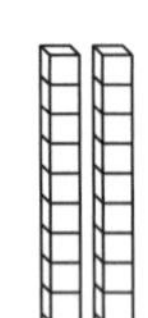
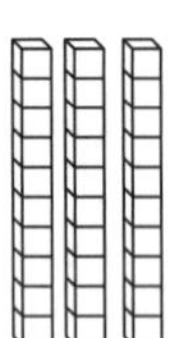

____, ____, ____

❺ Circle the shape that does not belong.

❻ This month is ____________.

❼

____ + ____ = ____

Double 5 = ____

❽ Write about the number 5.

5 is 1 less than ____.

5 is 1 more than ____.

5 is 3 combined with ____.

5 is 2 groups of 2 plus ____.

5 is double 2 plus ____.

❾ 3 + 4 = ____ 5 + 3 = ____

4 + 2 = ____ 6 + 3 = ____

4 + 4 = ____ 7 + 2 = ____

❿ Make the numbers at the bottom add to give 7.

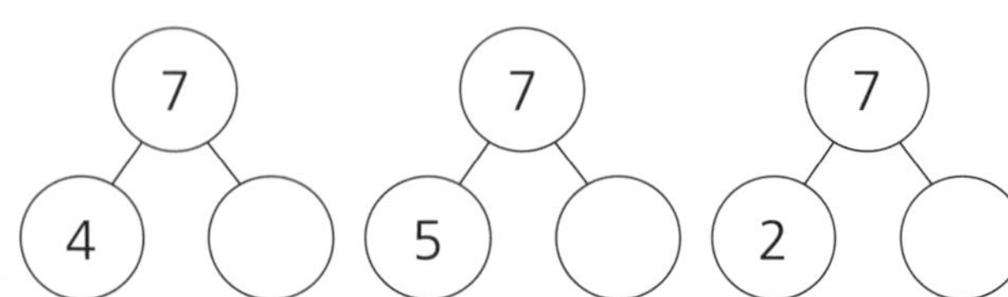

 • *AUSTRALIAN SIGNPOST MATHS 1 MENTALS* • ISBN 978 0 6557 0881 0

18:2

Double 3 = ☐

1. The pencils are in bundles of 10. How many in each group?

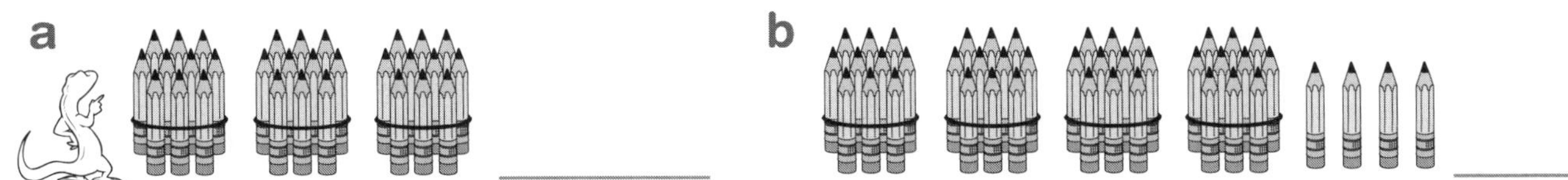

a ______ b ______

2. Write the months in the correct order.

May August January March July October
September June November February April December

1 ______ 2 ______ 3 ______

4 ______ 5 ______ 6 ______

7 ______ 8 ______ 9 ______

10 ______ 11 ______ 12 ______

18:3

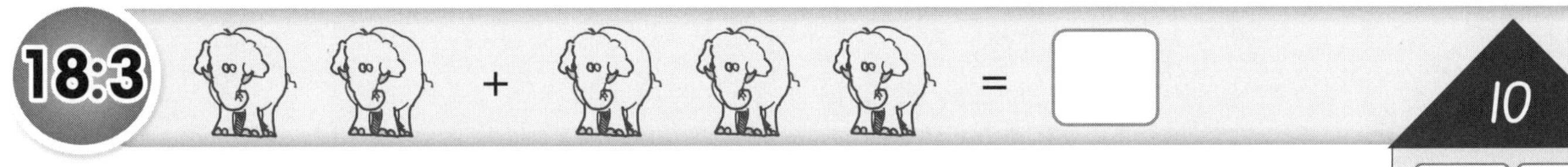

1. Complete each number bond house.

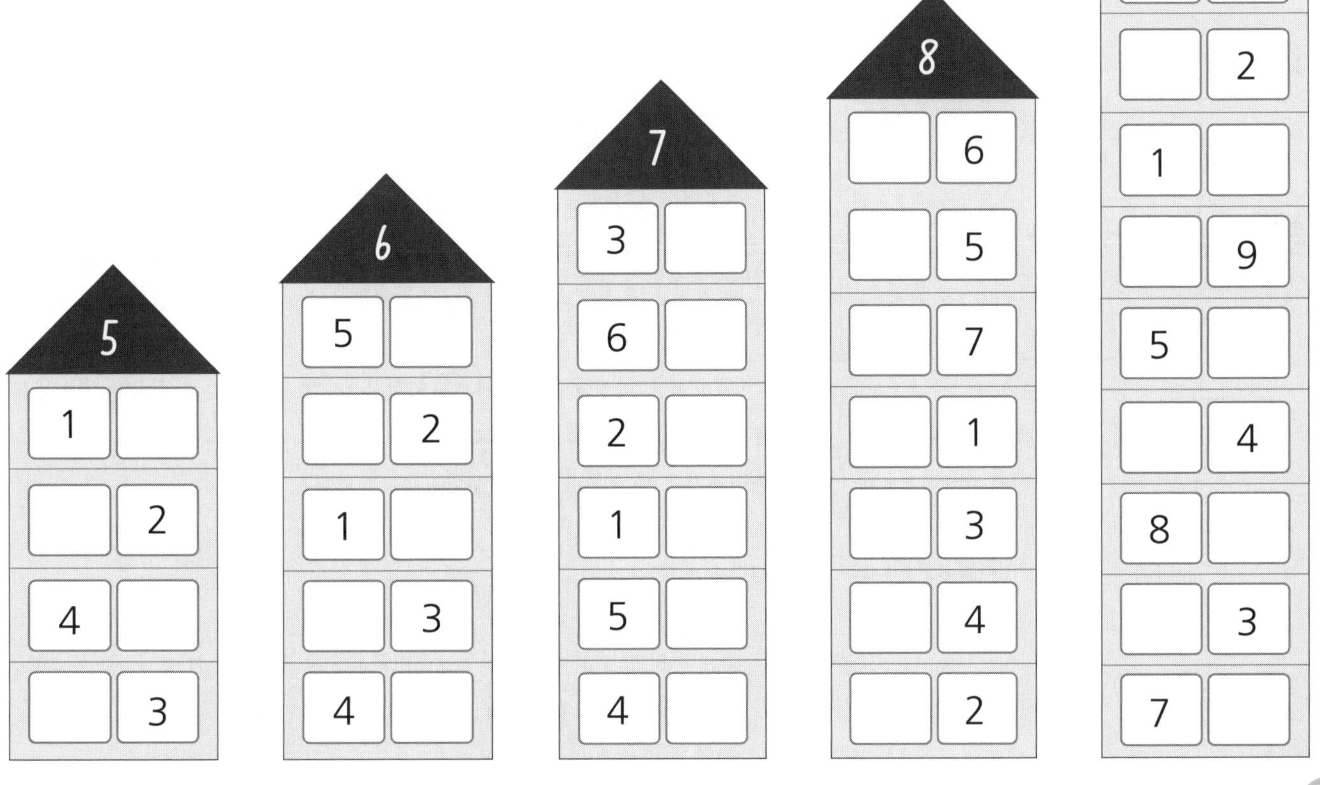

 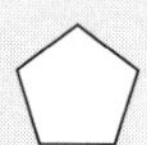 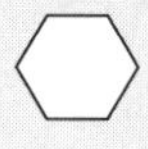 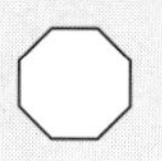

1 How many more squares? ____

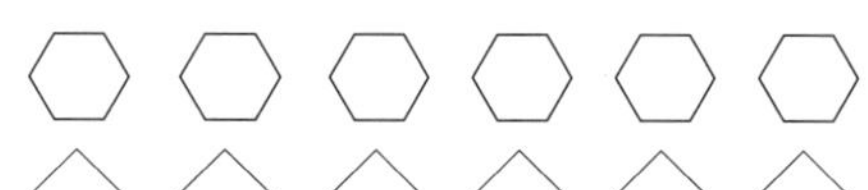

8 – 6 = ____

2 A pentagon has ____ sides and ____ vertices.

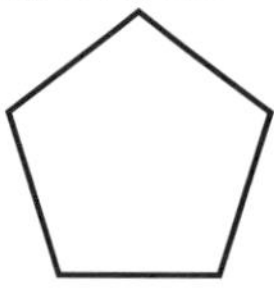

An octagon has ____ sides and ____ vertices.

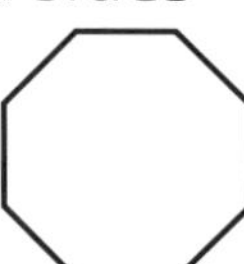

3 Make the numbers at the bottom add to give 8.

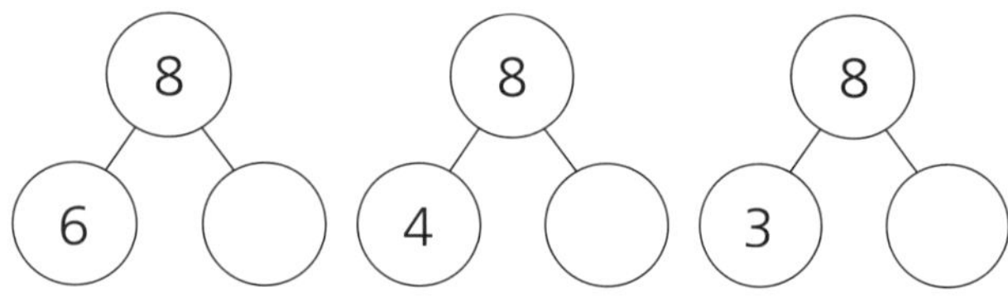

4 5 + 5 = ____ 4 + 4 = ____

4 + 2 = ____ 7 + 2 = ____

5 What comes **before** and **after**?

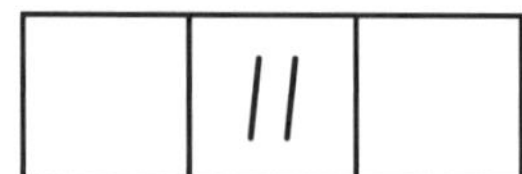

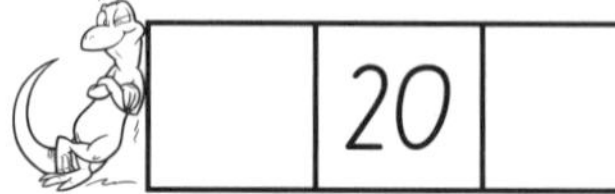

	28	

6 

The time shown is ____________.

7 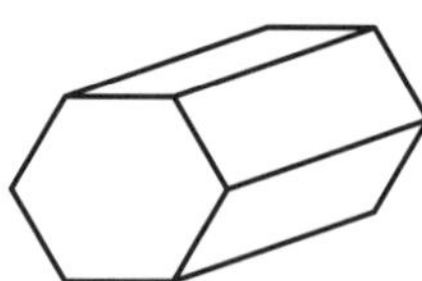

Name two shapes that are the faces of this 3D object.

____

____

8 Complete the number pattern. How many bells in each column?

 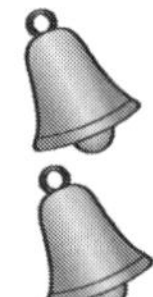 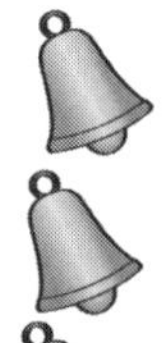 

____, ____, ____, ____

The rule is add ____.

9 Show:

a quarter to 4

a quarter past 2

Tick when done.

- [ ] In your head, count by tens to 100.
- [ ] In your head, count back by tens from 100 to 0.

 • *AUSTRALIAN SIGNPOST MATHS 1 MENTALS* • ISBN 978 0 6557 0881 0

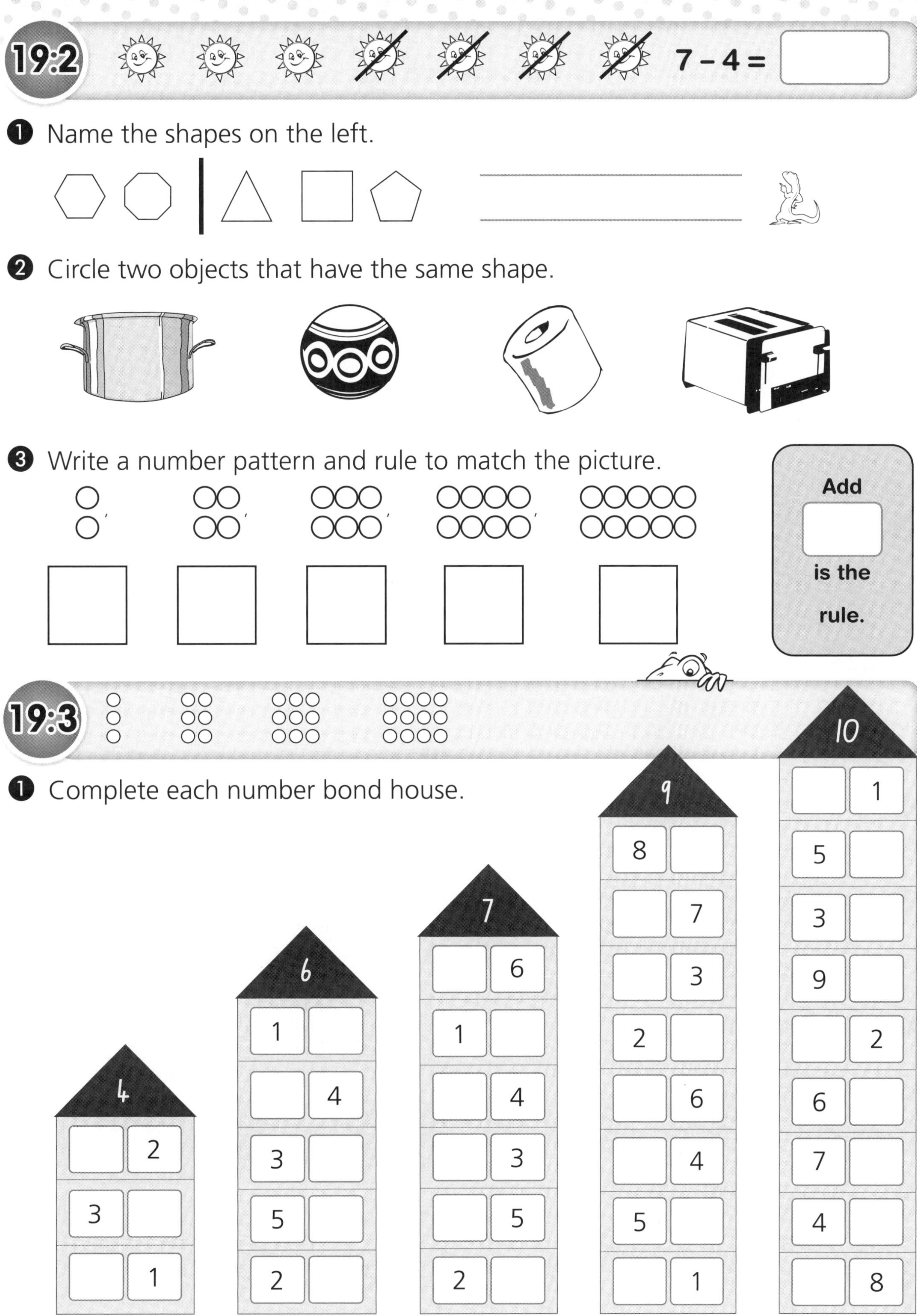
19:2
7 – 4 =
1 Name the shapes on the left.
2 Circle two objects that have the same shape.
3 Write a number pattern and rule to match the picture.
Add
is the
rule.
19:3
1 Complete each number bond house.
4
2
3
1
6
1
4
3
5
2
7
6
1
4
3
5
2
9
8
7
3
2
6
4
5
1
10
1
5
3
9
2
6
7
4
8

1. How many more hexagons? ______

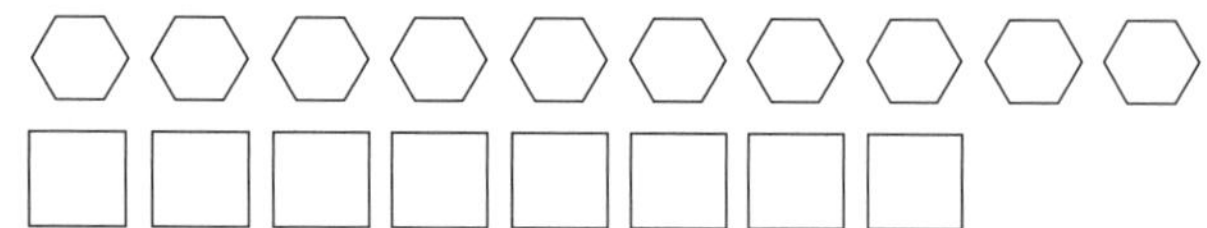

10 – ______ = ______

2. An octagon has ______ sides and ______ vertices.

3.

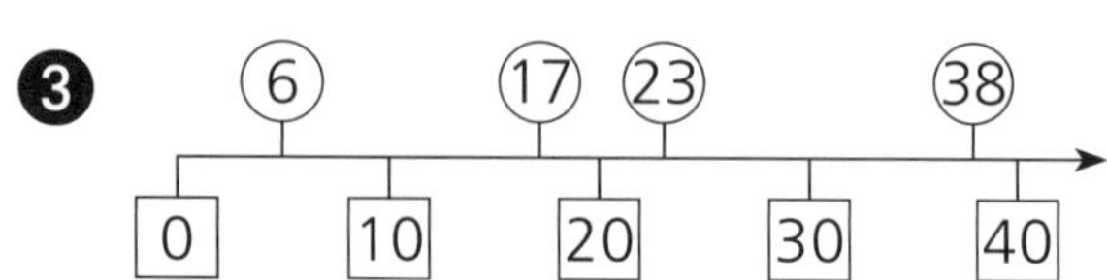

Write the nearest 10 to:

a 6 ______ **b** 17 ______

c 23 ______ **d** 38 ______

4. | 7 | tens | 9 | ones | ______

5. The number one more than:

20 ______ 33 ______

6. Write the numeral for:

a seventy-nine ______

b forty ______

c eighty-three ______

d one hundred and eight ______

7. Circle the smaller number.

89 or 98

8. Name two shapes that are faces of this 3D object.

______

______

9. Write a number bigger than 90. ______

10. 56 = ______ tens ______ ones

72 = ______ tens ______ ones

11. 6 + 4 = ______ 4 + 6 = ______

6 + 5 = ______ 5 + 6 = ______

Tick when done.

☐ Practise saying the friends of 10 in your head.

1 + 9 = 10 2 + 8 = 10
3 + 7 = 10 4 + 6 = 10
5 + 5 = 10 6 + 4 = 10
7 + 3 = 10 8 + 2 = 10
9 + 1 = 10

 AUSTRALIAN SIGNPOST MATHS 1 MENTALS • ISBN 978 0 6557 0881 0

20:2

○ ○ ○ + △ △ △ + ▭ ▭ ▭ = ▭

❶ Complete the numeral expander and then write the number.

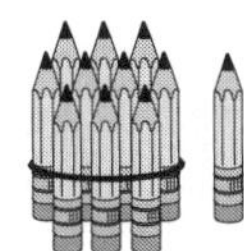

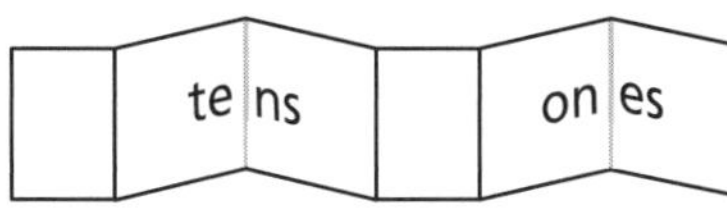

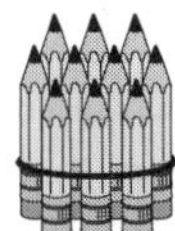
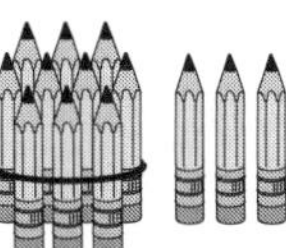
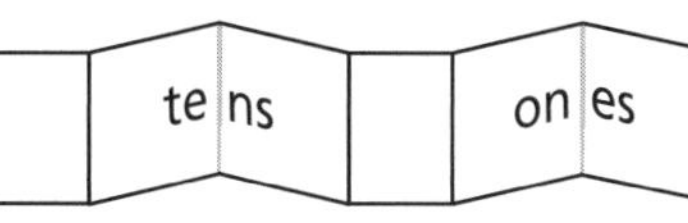

______ ______

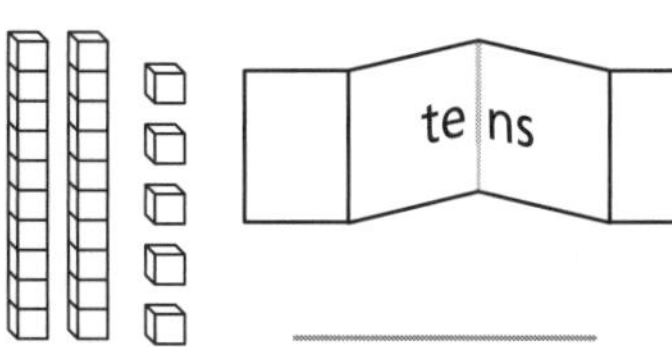

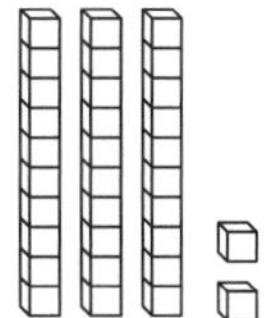
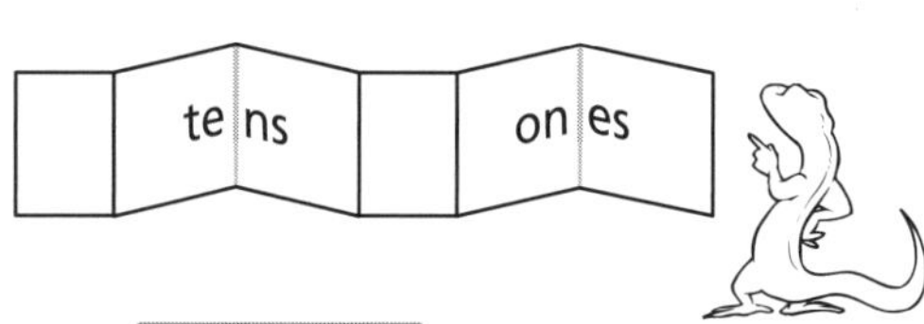

______ ______

❷ Write the missing numbers.

a 10, 20, 30, ____, ____, 60, ____, ____, ____, 100, ____, ____

b 74, 75, 76, ____, ____, ____, ____, 81, ____, ____, ____, ____

c 47, 48, 49, ____, ____, ____, ____, ____, 55, ____, ____, ____

20:3

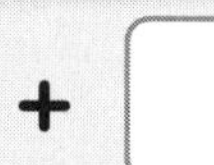

4 + ▭ = ▭

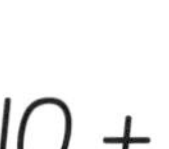

❶ Use the number line to count on and find:

a 8 + 3 = ____	**b** 9 + 4 = ____	**c** 10 + 2 = ____
d 8 + 6 = ____	**e** 10 + 4 = ____	**f** 11 + 4 = ____
g 9 + 2 = ____	**h** 8 + 4 = ____	**i** 8 + 5 = ____
j 8 + 7 = ____	**k** 9 + 3 = ____	**l** 9 + 5 = ____
m 10 + 3 = ____	**n** 9 + 6 = ____	**o** 10 + 5 = ____
p 11 + 5 = ____	**q** 12 + 3 = ____	**r** 13 + 3 = ____

21:1       ☐ + ☐ = ☐

1. 82 = _____ tens _____ ones

   46 = _____ tens _____ ones

2. Write the name for:

   a 29 ____________________

   b 18 ____________________

3. 

   6 + _____ = 10

   10 – 6 = _____

4. 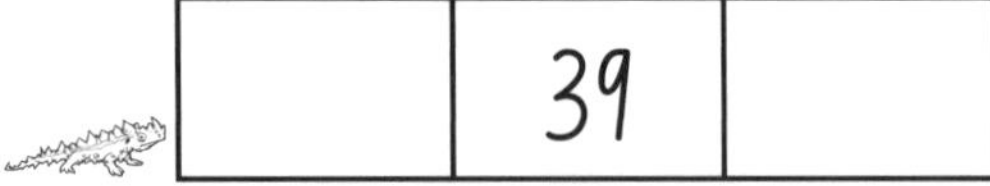

7	tens	4	ones

   _____

5. Write the number before and after 39.

	39	

6. ← 3 4 5 6 7 8 9 10 →

   The difference between 5 and 8 is _____.

7. Write the numeral for:

   a ten _____ **b** twenty _____

   c twelve _____ **d** thirteen _____

8. Circle to match the sphere to an object.

   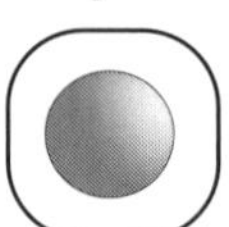   

9. | 5 | tens | 1 | ones |
   |---|---|---|---|

   _____

10. Draw more balls to make 10.

    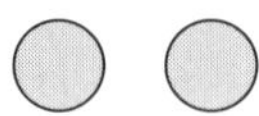

    5 + _____ = 10

    10 – 5 = _____

11. What number is shown? _____

    What number comes next? _____

12. 8 + 4 = _____ 9 + 2 = _____

13. 10, 20, 30, _____, _____

    90, 80, 70, _____, _____

Tick when done.

☐ Practise counting forwards and backwards by ones from any 2-digit number.

 • *AUSTRALIAN SIGNPOST MATHS 1 MENTALS* • ISBN 978 0 6557 0881 0

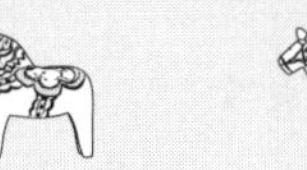   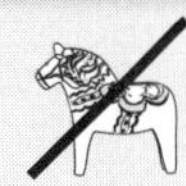 5 – 3 = ☐

❶ Tick after counting by:

2s to 50 ☐

5s to 50 ☐

10s to 50 ☐

❷ Start at any number. Count forwards or backwards by ones.

1	2	3	4	5	6	7	8	9	10
11	12	13	14	15	16	17	18	19	20
21	22	23	24	25	26	27	28	29	30
31	32	33	34	35	36	37	38	39	40
41	42	43	44	45	46	47	48	49	50

❸ Use the number chart to find the nearest ten to each number.

a 32 _____ **b** 8 _____ **c** 44 _____ **d** 27 _____ **e** 49 _____

❹ Write these numbers in order, starting with the smallest.

20, _____, _____, _____, _____

21:3

        +  = 

❶ Complete these number cards.

a

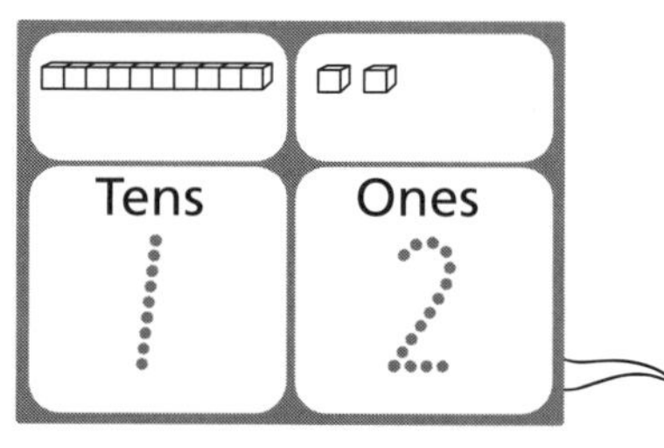

b

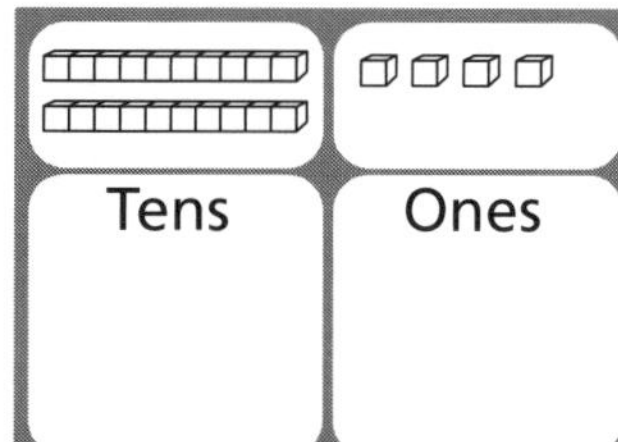

c

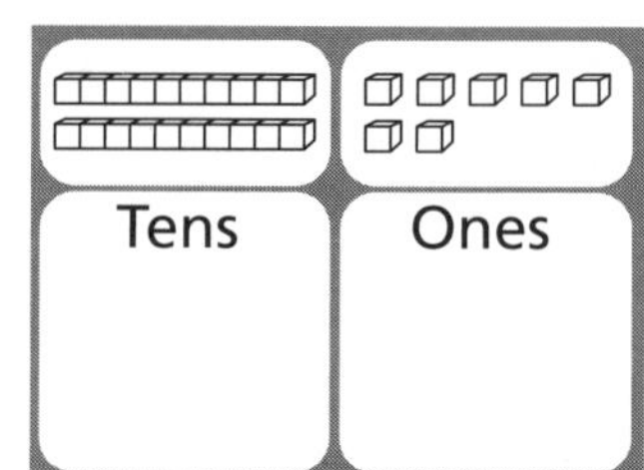

d

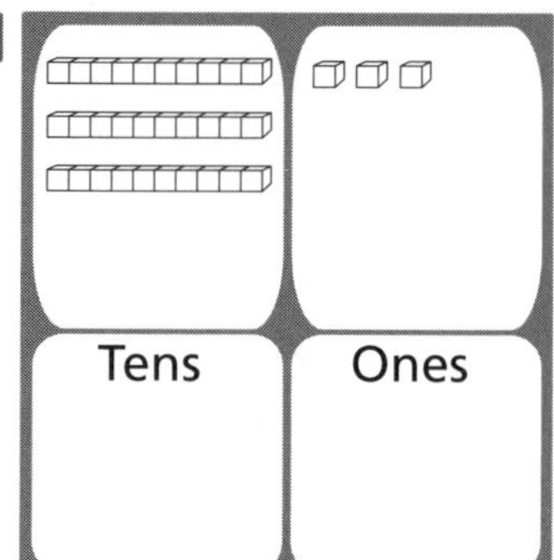

e

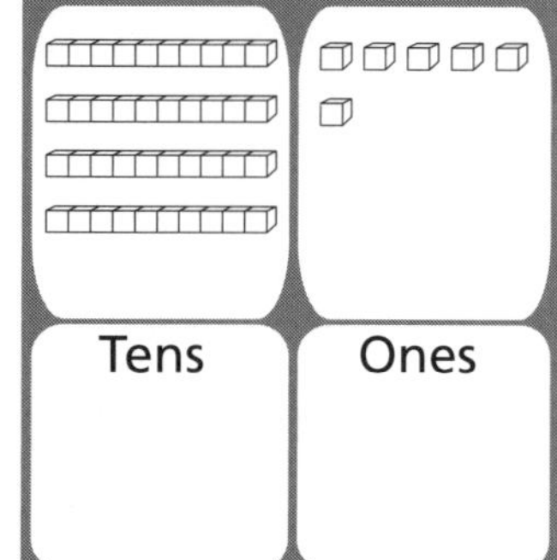

f

Tens | Ones

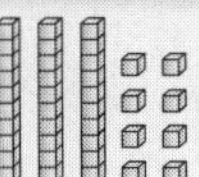

1. 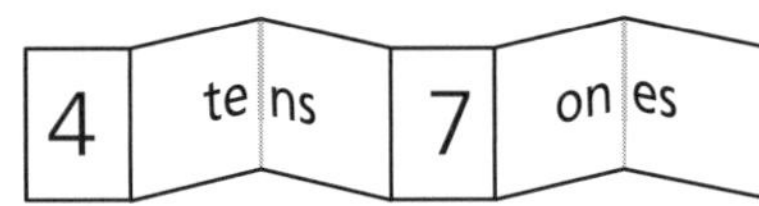

______

2. Write the number on each abacus.

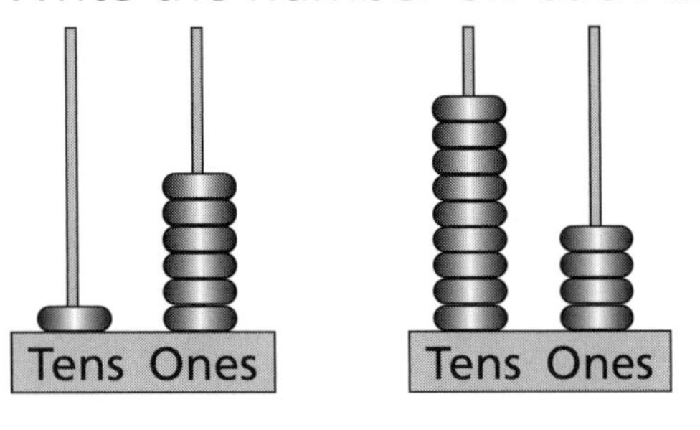

______ ______

3. Which number in Question 2 is larger? ______

4.     

____ groups of ____ = ____

____ + ____ + ____ + ____ = ____

5. Circle the smaller number.

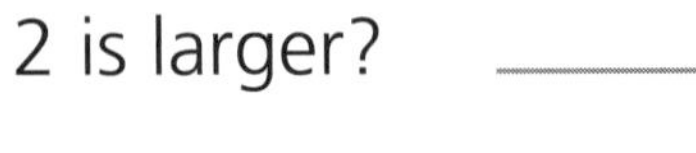

6. Draw stars to make equal groups.

  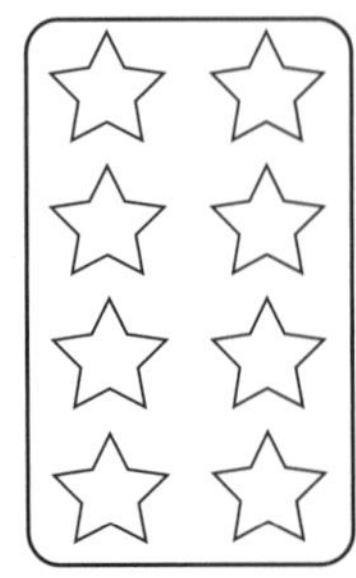

_____ groups of _____ = _____

7. Draw more balls to make 9.

6 + ____ = 9

9 – 6 = ____

8. Match each 3D object to a picture.

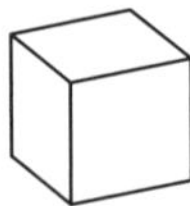 

9. Circle groups of 2.

How many lollies? _____

How many groups of 2? _____

10. How many blocks were used to make each model?

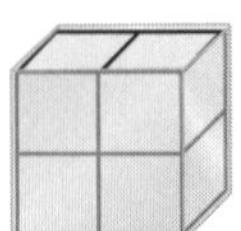 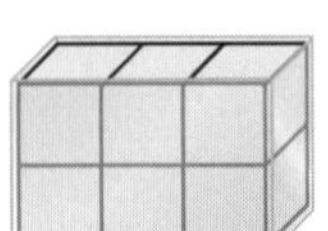 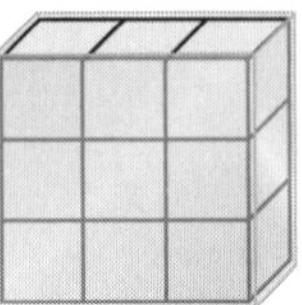

______ ______ ______

Tick when done.

☐ Start at 0. Count by 2s until you get to 40.

 • *AUSTRALIAN SIGNPOST MATHS 1 MENTALS* • ISBN 978 0 6557 0881 0

22:2

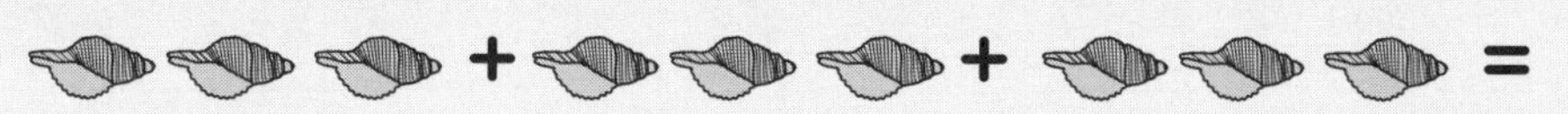

❶ Draw circles to show these groups.

a groups of 3 flowers

3 + 3 + 3 + 3 = _____

How many flowers? _____

How many groups of 3? _____

b groups of 2 pencils

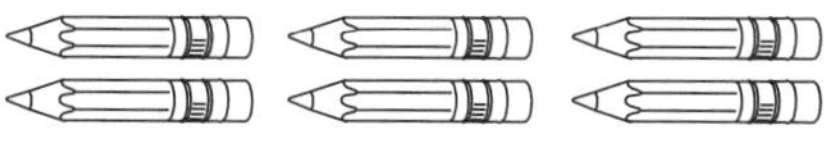

2 + 2 + 2 = _____

How many pencils? _____

How many groups of 2? _____

❷ Amir has _____ cars.

Anika has _____ cars.

How many more cars has Amir? _____

❸ 5 + _____ = 8   8 − 5 = _____

22:3

❶ Complete these number cards.

a

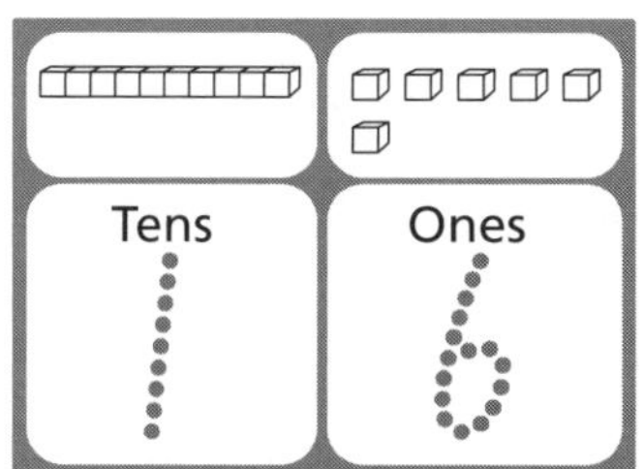

b

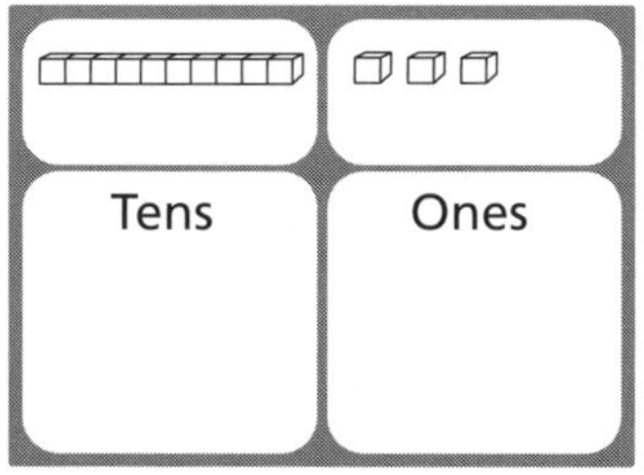

c

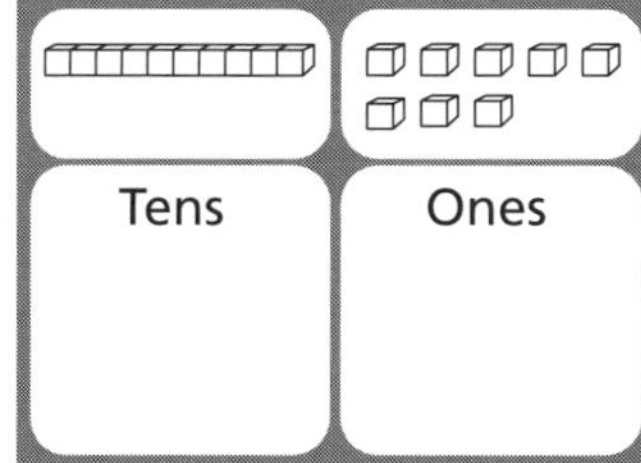

d

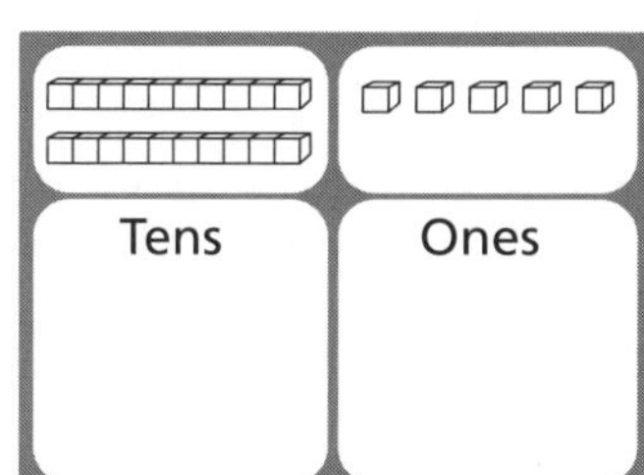

e

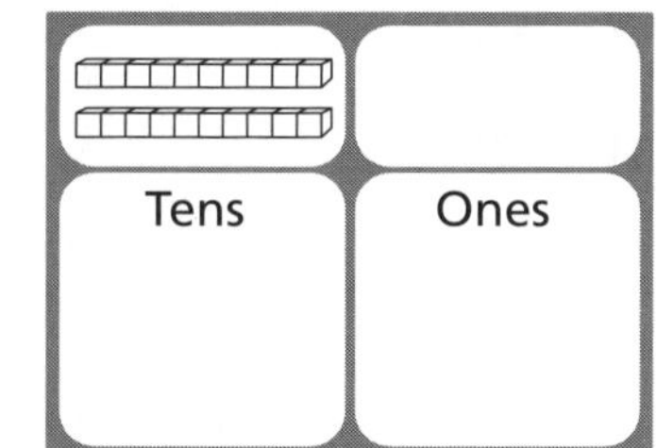

f

Tens	Ones

23:1 2, 4, 6, ____, ____, ____, ____, ____, ____

1 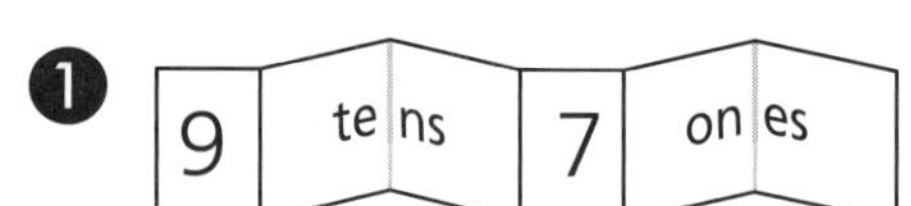 ____

2 Write the numeral for:

seventy-three ____

ninety-one ____

3 Circle the larger number.

a 36 or 63

b 90 or 87

4 Circle groups of 3.

How many berries? ____

How many groups of 3? ____

5 **a** 5, 10, 15, ____, ____, ____

b 90, 80, 70, ____, ____, ____

6 45 = ____ tens ____ ones

7   

____ groups of ____ cats

= ____ cats altogether.

8 Order the areas (1, 2, 3) from smallest to largest.

  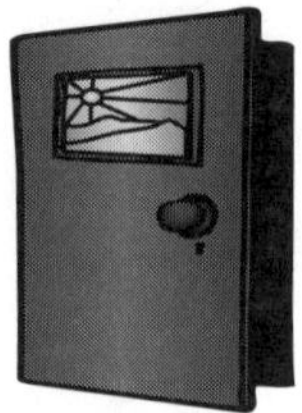

t-shirt ____ stamp ____ door ____

9 How many blocks were used to make each model?

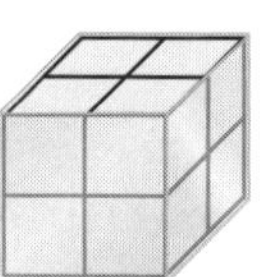  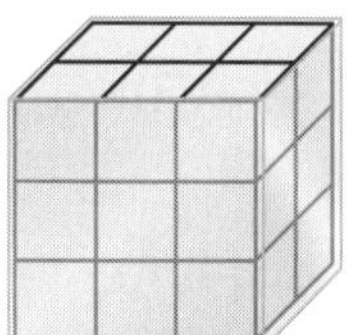

____ ____ ____

10 Write the number before and after.

	71	

Tick when done.

☐ Learn these near doubles:

$6 + 5 = 1 + (5 + 5)$ $= 1 + 10$ $= 11$	$7 + 6 = 1 + (6 + 6)$ $= 1 + 12$ $= 13$
$8 + 7 = 1 + (7 + 7)$ $= 1 + 14$ $= 15$	$9 + 8 = 1 + (8 + 8)$ $= 1 + 16$ $= 17$

23:2

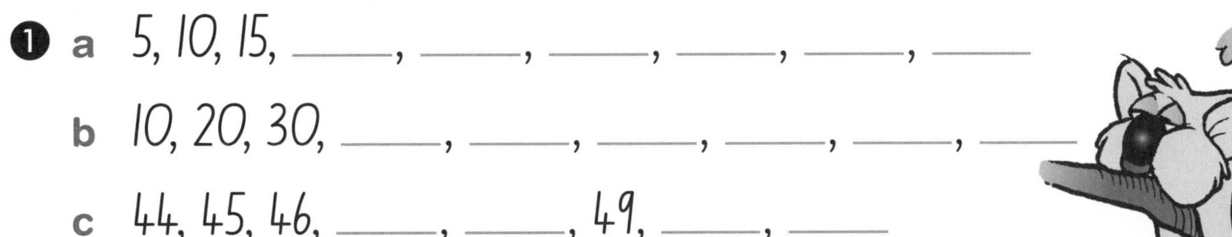

❶ a 5, 10, 15, ____, ____, ____, ____, ____, ____

b 10, 20, 30, ____, ____, ____, ____, ____, ____

c 44, 45, 46, ____, ____, 49, ____, ____

d 67, 68, ____, 70, ____, 72, ____, ____

❷ Draw circles to show these groups.

a groups of 2 spoons

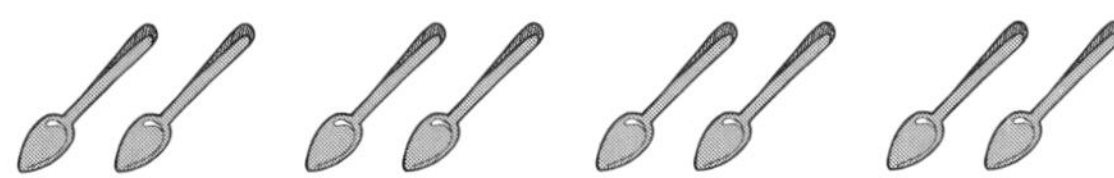

2 + 2 + 2 + 2 = ____

How many spoons? ____

How many groups of 2? ____

b groups of 4 guitars

4 + 4 = ____

How many guitars? ____

How many groups of 4? ____

❸ a The month **after** August is ____________.

b 1 year = ____ months

23:3

5, 10, 15, ____, ____, ____, ____, ____, ____

❶ Finish each number pattern.

a 2, 4, ____, 8, ____

b 1, 3, ____, ____, 9

c 10, 8, ____, ____, 2

d 5, 7, ____, ____, 13

e 6, 8, ____, ____, 14

f 9, 7, ____, ____, 1

g 14, 12, ____, ____, 6

h 13, 11, ____, ____, 5

24:1 10, 20, 30, 40, ____, ____, ____, ____, ____, ____

❶ a 83, 84, 85, ____, ____, ____

b 64, 65, 66, ____, ____, ____

c 10, 20, 30, ____, ____, ____

d 70, 60, 50, ____, ____, ____

e 2, 4, 6, ____, ____, ____

f 50, 45, 40, ____, ____, ____

❷ How many blocks were used to make each model?

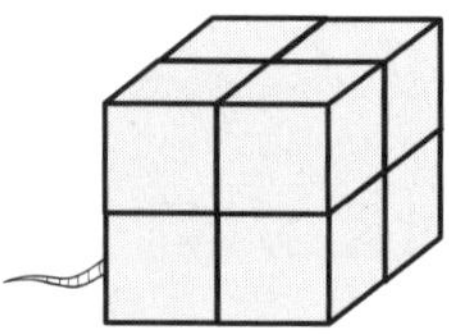 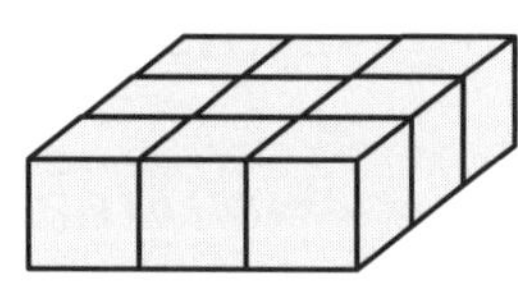

____ ____

❸ Draw more lollies to make four fair shares.

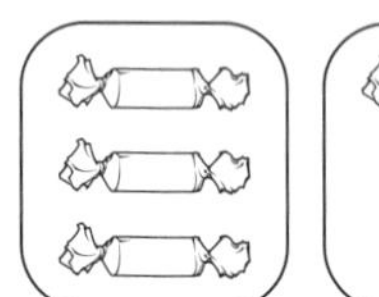 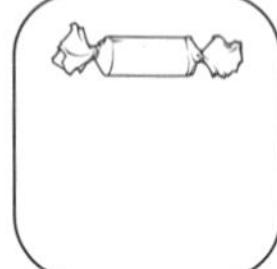 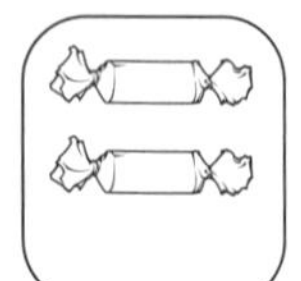 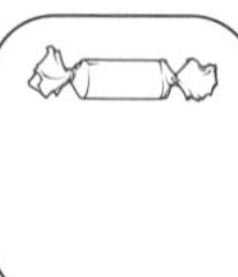

3, 6, ____, ____

4 groups of 3 = ____

❹ Write the missing numbers.

a 56, ____, 58, ____, 60

b 42, ____, 44, ____, 46

❺ Circle groups of five faces.

How many groups of 5? ____

5, 10, ____, ____, ____

There are ____ faces above.

❻ Mark each angle with a dot.

How many angles in each shape?

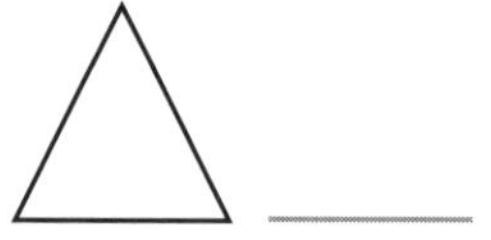 ____  ____

❼ Circle the item with the smaller area.

a tea towel a bed sheet

❽ Draw 3 groups of 2 circles.

Tick when done.

Start at 0 each time.

☐ Count by 5s until you get to 50.

☐ Count by 2s until you get to 20.

☐ Count by 10s until you get to 100.

24:2

, ☐ groups of ☐ = ☐

❶ Draw a line of symmetry for each picture.

  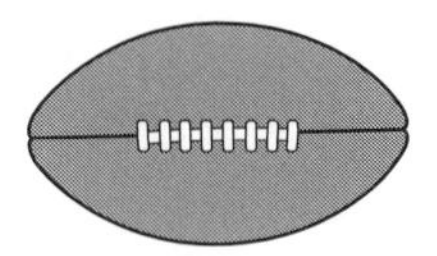 

❷ **a** 5, 10, 15, ______, ______, ______, 35, ______, ______, 50, ______, ______

b 0, 10, 20, ______, ______, ______, 60, ______, ______, 90, ______, ______

❸ Write the numeral for each.

a thirty-two ______ **b** seventy-four ______

c fifteen ______ **d** one hundred and eight ______

e fifty ______ **f** twenty-one ______

❹ Count on to find the answers.

3 + 2 = ____ 13 + 2 = ____ 8 + 1 = ____ 18 + 1 = ____

5 + 4 = ____ 15 + 4 = ____ 6 + 3 = ____ 16 + 3 = ____

24:3

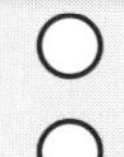 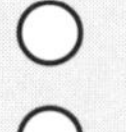    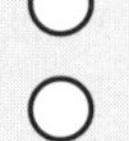

☐ groups of 2

❶ Complete each number web.

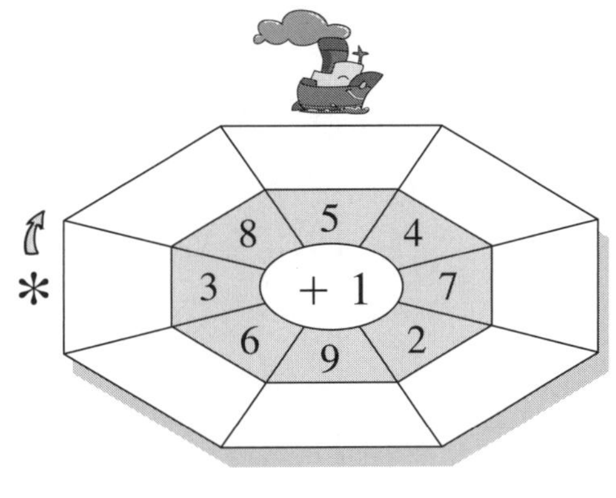

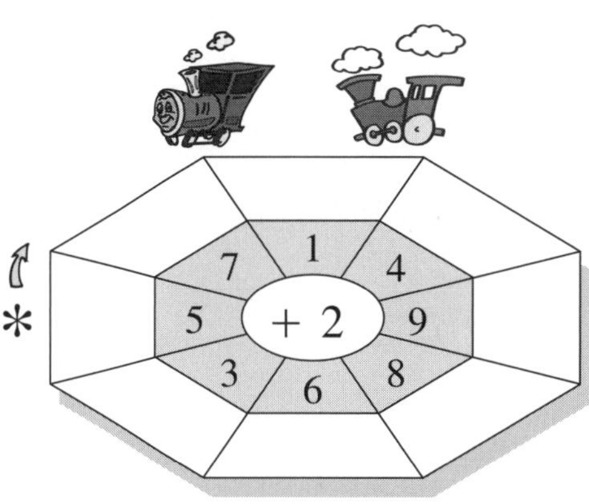

25:1 ____, 24, 25, ____ / 57, 58, ____, ____

1 20, 22, 24, ____, ____

2, 4, 6, ____, ____, ____

2 How many blocks were used to make each model?

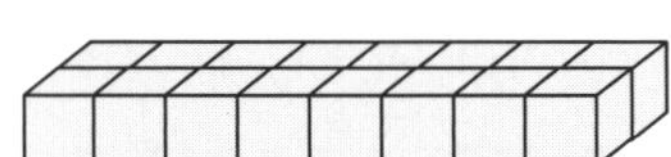

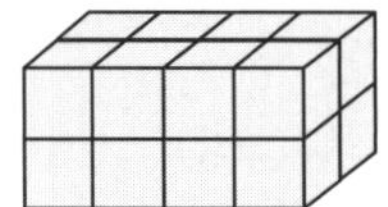

____ ____

3 Mark each angle with a dot.

How many angles in each shape?

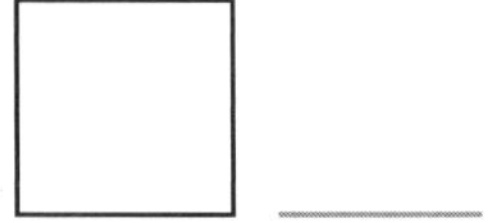 ____

 ____

4 Skip count by twos to find:

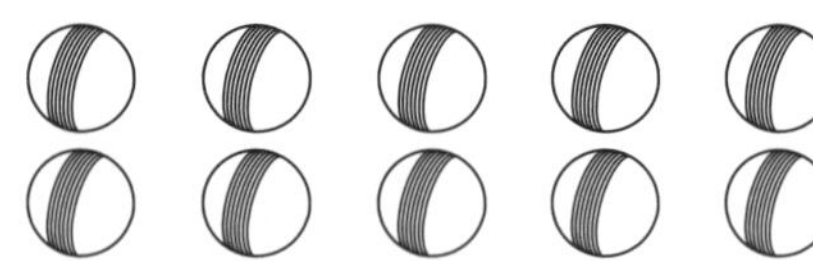

2 groups of 2 ____

4 groups of 2 ____

3 groups of 2 ____

5 Finish the pattern and write the rule.

3, 6, 9, ____, ____, ____

The rule is add ____.

6 a How many groups? ____

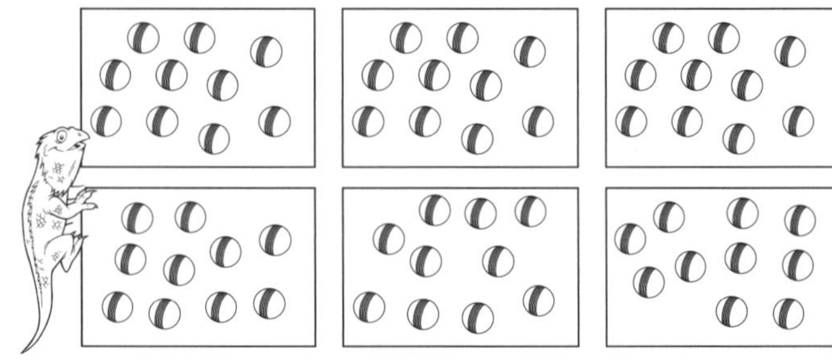

b How many in each group? ____

c Skip count to find the total.

10, 20, 30, ____, ____, ____

d There are ____ balls.

7 Read a book. Draw a counter every time you see one of these words. Keep going until one line is full.

and					
it					
the					

Which word was most popular?

____

8 6 + 2 = ____ 4 + 2 = ____

Tick when done.

☐ Count by 10s from 10 to 100.

☐ Count by 2s from 10 to 20.

☐ Count by 5s from 10 to 40.

January, February, March, April, May, June, July, August, September, October, November, December

❶ Draw a line of symmetry for each.

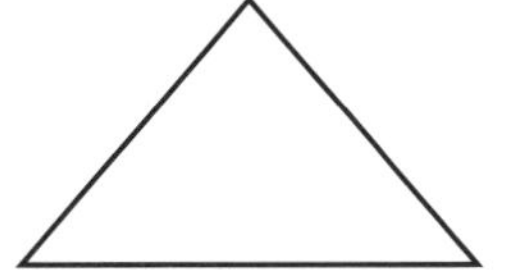   

❷ In which months do these events happen?

Anzac Day

____

Mother's Day

____

Christmas

____

❸ **a** How many months in one year? ________

b What is the fifth month? __________

c March is the ________ month.

d What is the last month of the year? ______________

e What month comes after February? Circle. **June / March**

f What month comes after June? Circle. **August / July**

❶ Complete each number web.

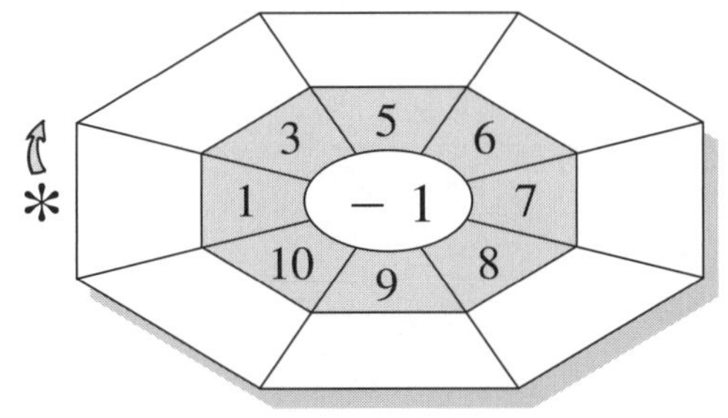

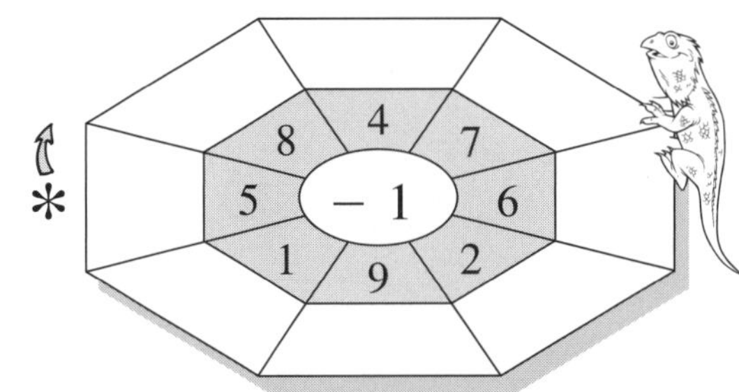

26:1

5, 10, 15, ______, ______, ______, ______, ______, ______

❶ Skip count by threes to find:

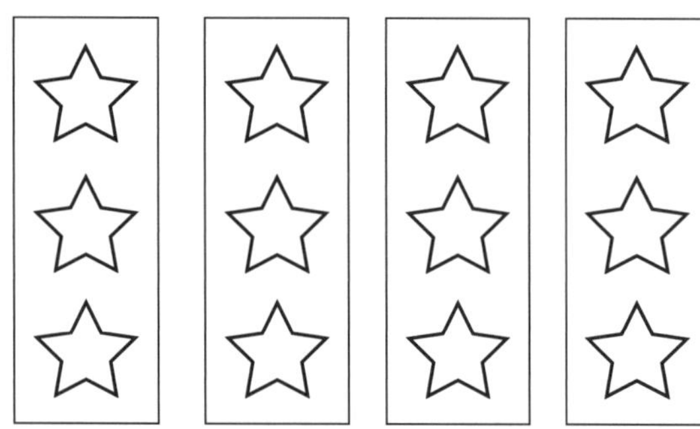

2 groups of 3 ______

4 groups of 3 ______

3 groups of 3 ______

❷ Name these shapes.

a 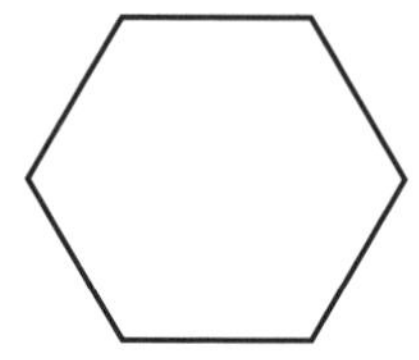

b 

______ ______

Sides: ______ ______

Vertices: ______ ______

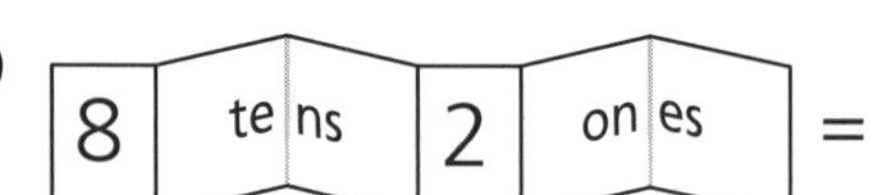

= ______

❹ Write the numeral for:

sixty-three ______

seventy-eight ______

❺ 4 + 6 = ______ 10 + 4 = ______

7 + 3 = ______ 10 + 7 = ______

❻ Write these numbers in order.

43, 27, 55, 17

______, ______, ______, ______

❼ 3 + 5 = ______ 5 + 3 = ______

❽ Finish the patterns.

a 7, 9, 11, 13, ______, ______

b 12, 10, 8, 6, ______, ______

c 40, 50, 60, ______, ______

❾ Write the rule for each part in Question 8.

a Rule: ______

b Rule: ______

c Rule: ______

❿ Write the time.

______

Tick when done.

- ☐ Count backwards by 10s from 90 to 0.
- ☐ Count backwards by 5s from 50 to 0.
- ☐ Count backwards by 2s from 20 to 0.

5, 15, 25, 35, _____, _____, _____, _____, _____, _____

1. Write in the missing months.

January, February, __________, __________, __________, June, __________, August, September, October, __________, December

2. Today is ________________. Tomorrow is ________________.

3.

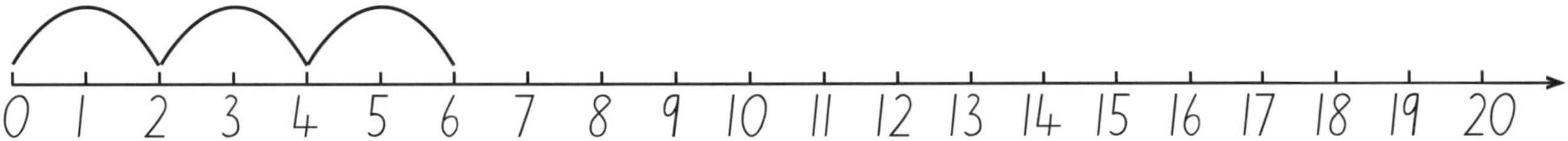

a Continue the number pattern on the number line and below.

0, 2, 4, 6, ____, ____, ____, ____, ____, ____, ____

b The repeating pattern in the ones place is ____________________.

Read this rhyme in your head three times. (Try to learn this rhyme.)

30 days has September, April, June and November. All the rest have 31 except February alone, which has 28 days clear and 29 days each leap year.

   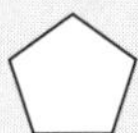 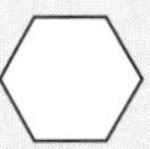 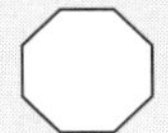 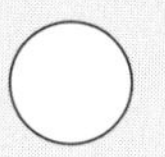

1. Start at the larger number. Count on to add.

3 + 2 = ____	6 + 3 = ____	4 + 6 = ____
5 + 4 = ____	1 + 7 = ____	1 + 8 = ____
10 + 0 = ____	2 + 6 = ____	7 + 3 = ____
8 + 3 = ____	5 + 5 = ____	6 + 2 = ____

2. Colour every 2nd bead, starting from the bottom right.

Start

20 10

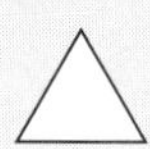  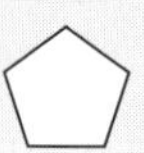 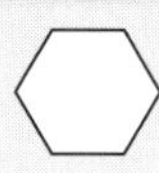 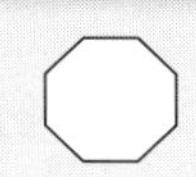

1. 5 + 2 = ____ 2 + 5 = ____

   5 + 2 = 2 + 5 = ____

2. 30, 29, 28, ____, ____

   3, 6, 9, ____, ____, ____

   30, 40, 50, ____, ____

   6, 16, 26, ____, ____

   10, 15, 20, ____, ____, ____

   16, 14, 12, ____, ____, ____

3. Name the shape below.

   ____

   ______ sides

   ______ vertices

   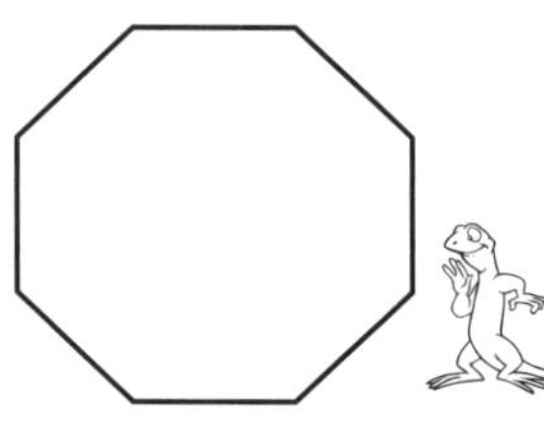

4. How many days are in September? ______

5. How many days are in one week? ______

6. 8 + 9 = ____ 9 + 8 = ____

7. This shape is a

   ______________________.

   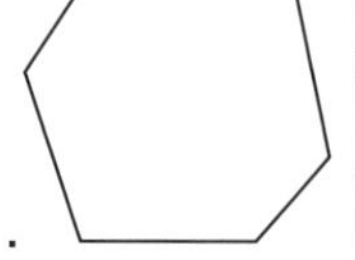

8.

February						
S	M	T	W	T	F	S
		1	2	3	4	5
6	7	8	9	10	11	12
13	14	15	16	17	18	19
20	21	22	23	24	25	26
27	28					

   a How many days in February? ______

   b On what day does February begin? ______

   c On what day does February end? ______

   d How many Saturdays in February? ______

9. 5 + 6 = ____ 6 + 5 = ____

   7 + 8 = ____ 8 + 7 = ____

10. Isaac can move 3 boxes on his trolley. How many boxes can he move if he makes:

   a 2 trips? ____ b 3 trips? ____

   c 4 trips? ____ d 5 trips? ____

Tick when done.

- [ ] Count by 2s from 2 to 20.
- [ ] Count by 10s from 10 to 100.
- [ ] Count by 5s from 5 to 50.
- [ ] Count by 3s from 3 to 30.

27:2

2, 4, 6, ____, ____, ____, ____, ____, ____, ____

1. 30 days has September, ____________, June and ________________.

All the rest have ____________, except ________________ alone,

which has ____________ days clear and ________ days each ________ year.

2. a Fill in the numbers for the first 22 days of November, for this year.

NOVEMBER						
Sunday	Monday	Tuesday	Wednesday	Thursday	Friday	Saturday

b Colour the first Wednesday. c Tick the 10th of November.

27:3

☐ groups of ☐ = ☐

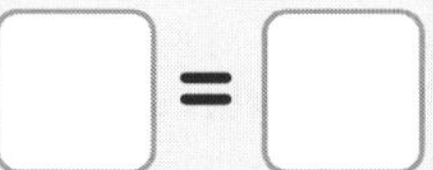

1. Count back to find:

10 – 6 = ____ 10 – 2 = ____ 10 – 4 = ____

10 – 5 = ____ 10 – 1 = ____ 10 – 8 = ____

10 – 7 = ____ 10 – 3 = ____ 10 – 9 = ____

2. Colour every 5th bead, starting from the bottom right.

Start

20 10

 • *AUSTRALIAN SIGNPOST MATHS 1 MENTALS* • ISBN 978 0 6557 0881 0

28:1

  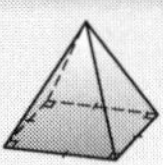  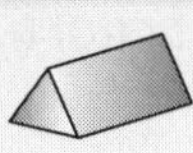 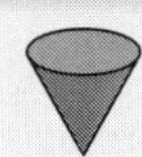 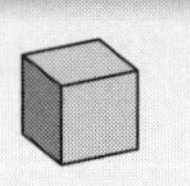

1. How many days are in November? ______

2. How many days are in one week? ______

3. Share 9 counters between the boxes.

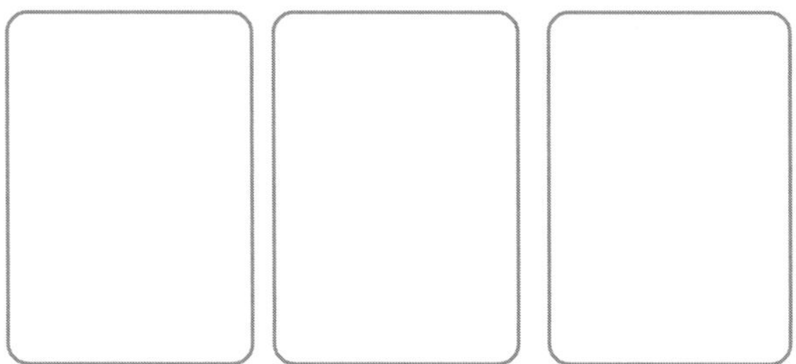

One share = ______________

4. 8 + 2 = _____ 2 + 8 = _____

5. Aarav was given bunches of cherries like this. How many cherries was he given if he was given:

a 2 bunches? _____

b 3 bunches? _____

c 4 bunches? _____

6. **a** Circle the objects that can stack.

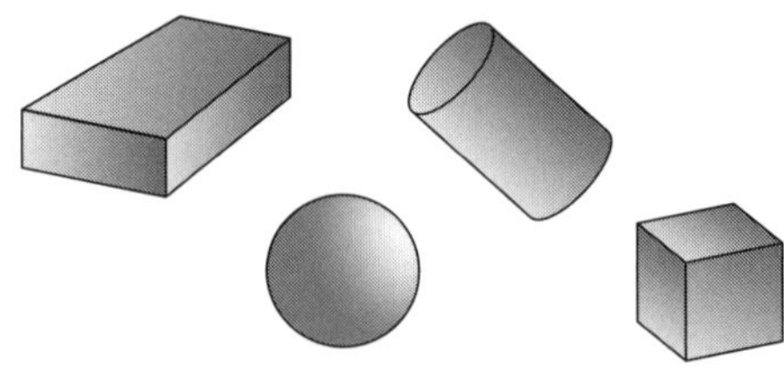

b Put a tick on the cube.

7. Follow the directions from Start.
Move 2 up, 2 right, 1 up, 3 left.

Where do you finish? _____

C			D
	E		
			B
	↑ Start		

8. Circle the model that has the least number of cubes.

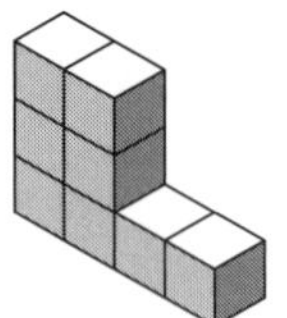 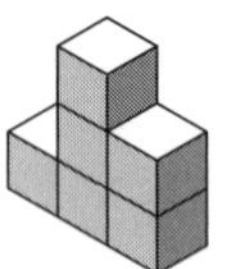 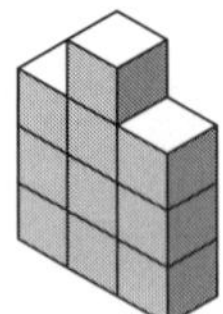

9. 8 + 4 = _____ 9 + 3 = _____

10 + 5 = _____ 8 + 3 = _____

Tick when done.

☐ Start counting from 1. See if you can get to 200.

28:2

January, February, March, April, May, June, July, August, September, October, November, December

1. a January, February, ________, ________, ________, June, ________, August, September, October, November, ________

 b Months in a year? ____ c Months in 2 years? ____

 Days in: d April? ____ e October? ____ f September? ____

 g Circle the 8th month of the year in the heading.

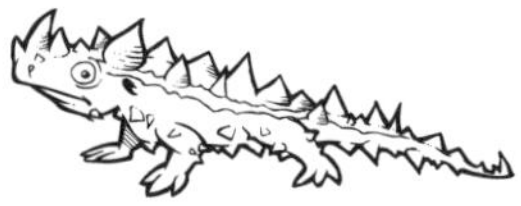

 h Put a cross on the 11th month of the year.

2. a Share 12 squares among 3 boxes. One share = ____ squares

 b Share 8 ovals among 4 boxes. One share = ____ ovals

28:3

0 2 4 6 8 10 12 14 16 18 20 22

1. Join the dots, counting by 2s.

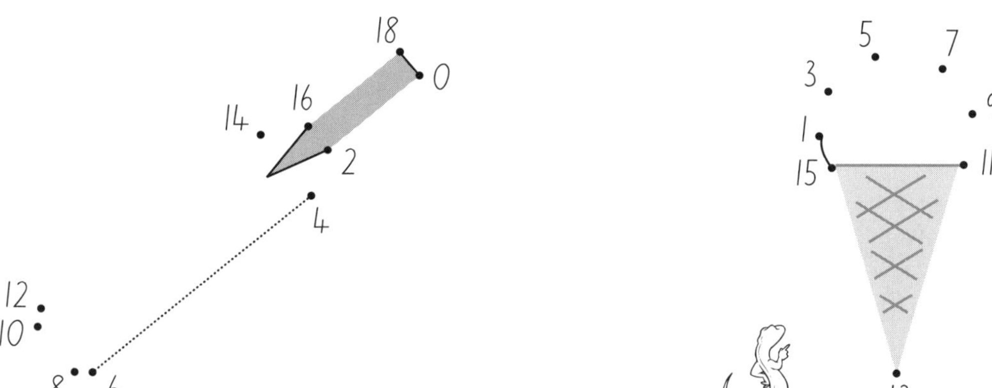

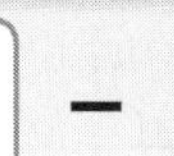

☐ – ☐ = ☐

1. Circle 4 groups of 2 dolphins.

2. Share 8 counters between the boxes.

One share = ______________

3. Circle the model with the most cubes.

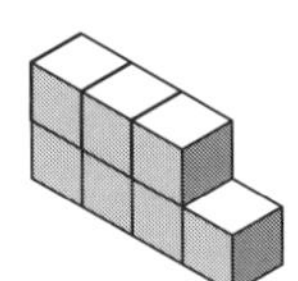
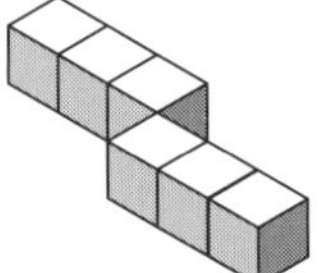
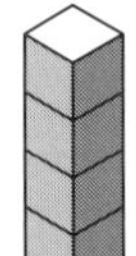

4. 

How many students could be given:

a 2 stars? ______________

b 3 stars? ______________

Tick when done.

☐ Say these in your head 10 times.

4 + 5 = 9   5 + 4 = 9

5. Do these two shapes have the same area? ______

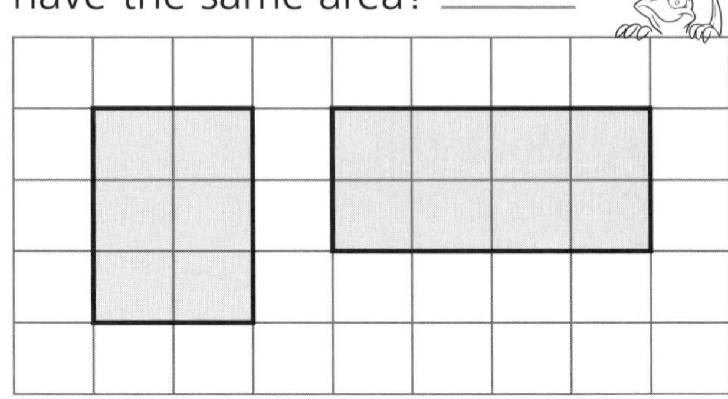

6. Draw two different shapes that have the same area.

7. 

How many of these books would cover this area? ______

8.

6 + 4 = ______   7 + 3 = ______

10 + 3 = ______   10 + 7 = ______

3 + 4 = ______   6 + 3 = ______

9 + 3 = ______   9 + 5 = ______

7 + 4 = ______   7 + 6 = ______

8 + 3 = ______   6 + 5 = ______

 ISBN 978 0 6557 0881 0

29:2

January, February, March, April, May, June, July, August, September, October, November, December

1 **a** Circle the months above that have 30 days.

b Underline the months that have 31 days.

2 Write the ordinal numbers.

first _____ second _____ third _____ fourth _____ fifth _____

3 

How many groups can you make if each group has:

a 4 hamburgers? _____ **b** 2 hamburgers? _____

c 3 hamburgers? _____ **d** 12 hamburgers? _____

29:3

 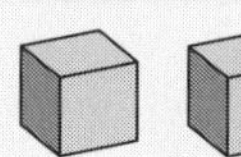   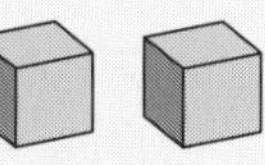 

☐ **groups of 2 =** ☐

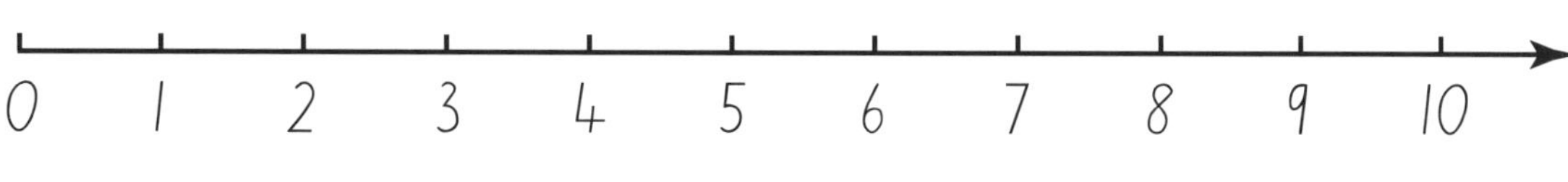

1 Use the number line to find:

8 – 4 = _____	9 – 6 = _____	10 – 5 = _____
3 – 3 = _____	5 – 0 = _____	10 – 4 = _____
9 – 2 = _____	7 – 1 = _____	10 – 7 = _____
9 – 3 = _____	8 – 2 = _____	10 – 6 = _____
5 – 2 = _____	9 – 5 = _____	10 – 3 = _____

1. Look for tens to find:

 a 4 + 7 + 6 + 3 = ____

 b 9 + 3 + 7 + 1 + 2 = ____

2. Share 12 counters between the boxes.

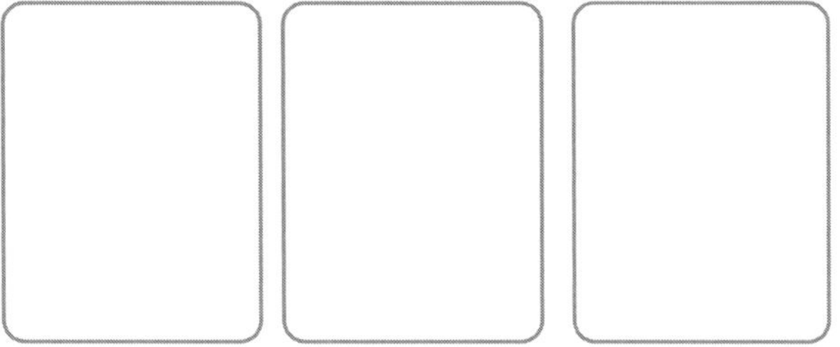

One share = ____

3. Colour the shape with the largest area.

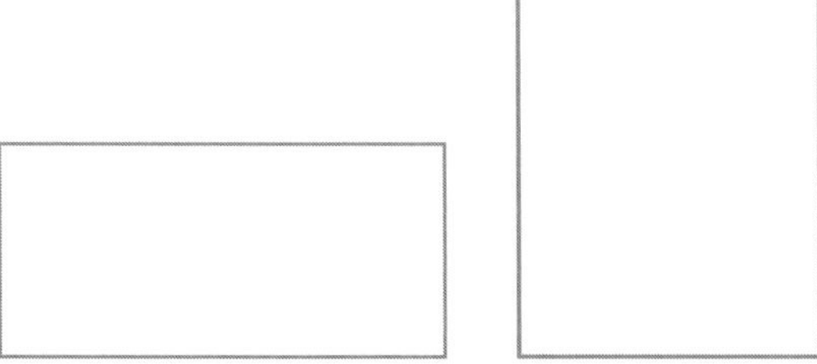

4. How many cubes? ____

5. 9 + 1 = ____   5 + 5 = ____

6.

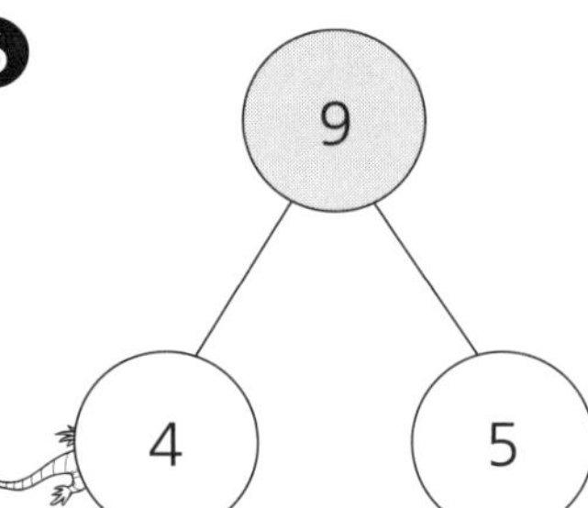

5 + 4 = ____

9 – 5 = ____

9 – 4 = ____

7.

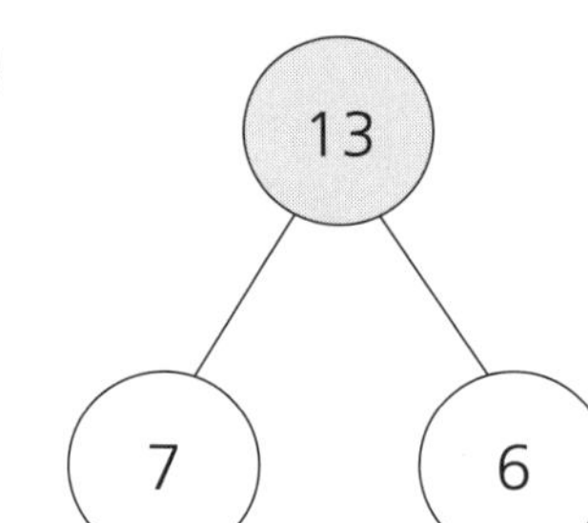

7 + 6 = ____

13 – 6 = ____

13 – 7 = ____

8.

How many students could be given:

 a 2 balls? ____

 b 3 balls? ____

9. Is this balanced, yes or no? ____

10. What is two less than twelve? ____

30:2

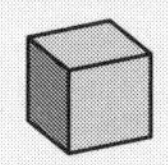  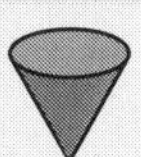    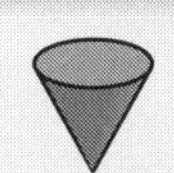

1 Look for tens to find:

a $8 + 6 + 4 + 2 =$ ____ **b** $5 + 3 + 5 + 7 + 6 =$ ____

2 **a**

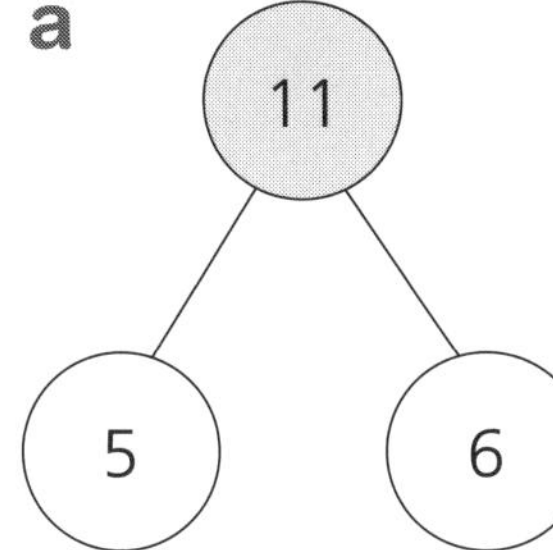

$5 + 6 =$ ____

$11 - 5 =$ ____

$11 - 6 =$ ____

b

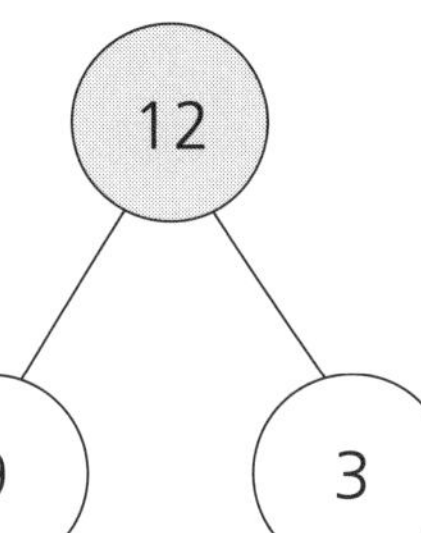

$9 + 3 =$ ____

$12 - 9 =$ ____

$12 - 3 =$ ____

3 Write the number 1 more than:

36 ____ 49 ____ 63 ____ 72 ____ 95 ____

30:3

1 3 5 7 9 11 13 15 17 19 21 23

1 Complete each number web.

a

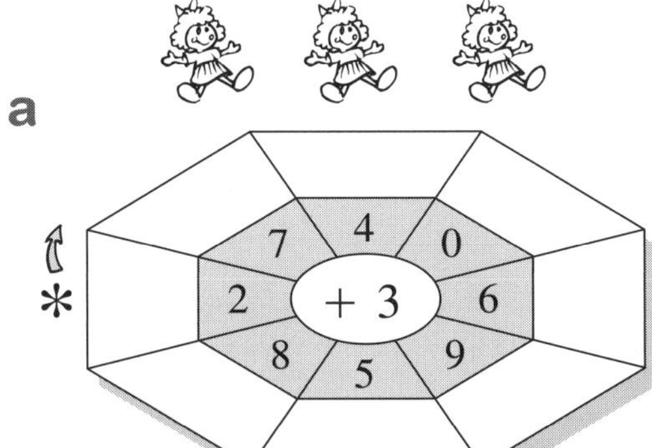

b

4
9
10
7
5
8
6
4
3
+ 4

c

5
6
7
8
9
10
11
2
– 2

d

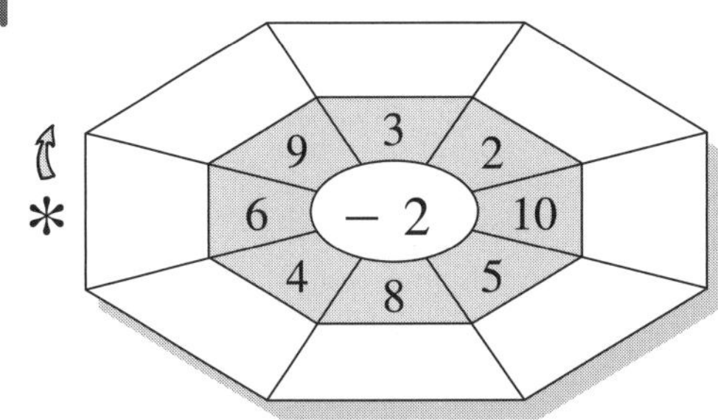

10, 15, 20, ____, ____, ____, ____, ____, ____

❶ Look for tens to find:

3	2	9	2
7	4	5	1
2	6	1	7
8	3	2	9
+ 1	+ 8	+ 5	+ 8
____	____	____	____

❷ 10 − 7 = ____

10 − 3 = ____

7 + 3 = ____

❸ Fill in the tens frame, then add the rest in the next tens frame.

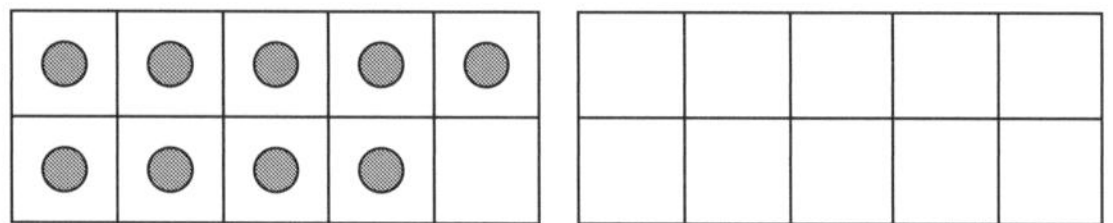

9 + 5 = 9 + ____ + ____

= 10 + ____ = ____

❹ Look for tens to find:

a 1 + 8 + 9 + 2 = ____

b 4 + 6 + 3 + 3 + 7 = ____

❺ Make a data display using these coins. One circle represents one coin.

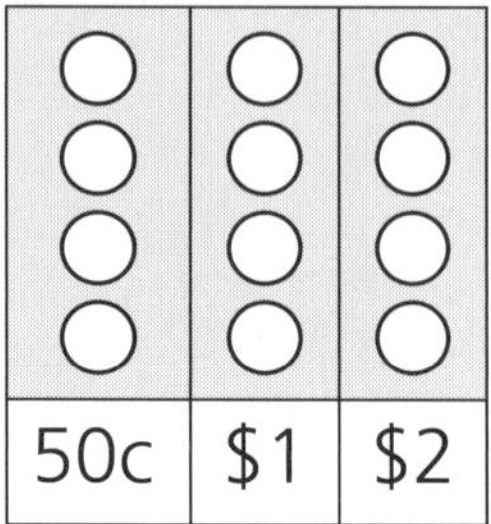

❻ Compare the mass of two objects by hefting.

The ____________ is heavier than the ____________.

❼ 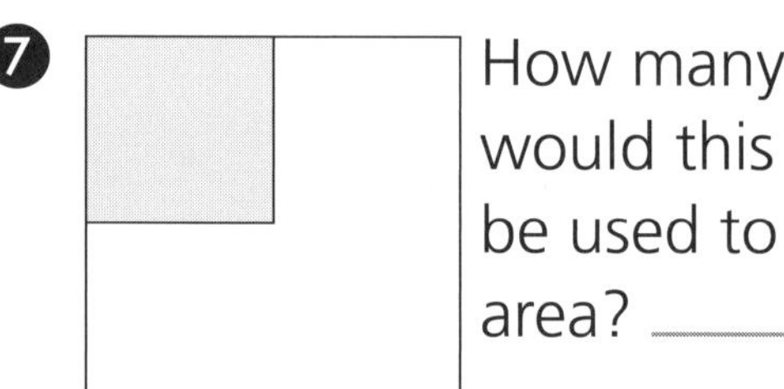
How many times would this square be used to cover this area? ________

❽ Write the ordinal numbers.

first ________ second ________

third ________ fourth ________

❾ 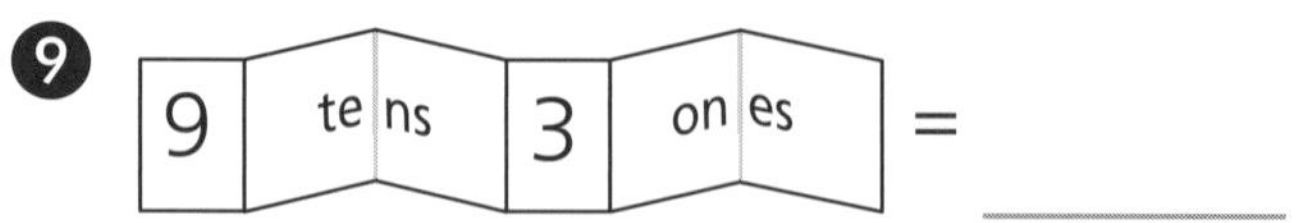

= ________

❿ Circle the biggest number.

33 24 61

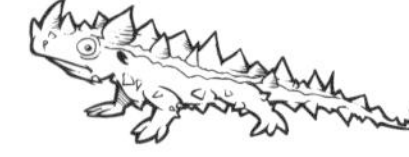

 ISBN 978 0 6557 0881 0

31:2

25 26 27 28 29 [30] 31 32 33 34 35 36 37

❶ Use the number line above to answer these by bridging to tens:

a 29 + 2 = ____ b 29 + 4 = ____ c 28 + 4 = ____

d 27 + 5 = ____ e 29 + 3 = ____ f 28 + 5 = ____

❷ Write the number 1 more than:

27 ____ 41 ____ 78 ____ 84 ____ 93 ____

❸ Continue these patterns.

a 36, 37, 38, ____, ____ b 22, 21, 20, ____, ____

c 10, 20, 30, ____, ____ d 2, 4, 6, ____, ____

31:3

 +  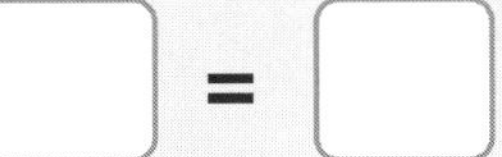 ☐ + ☐ = ☐

❶ Write the missing number to make the total in each number bond.
Complete the related number sentences.

a
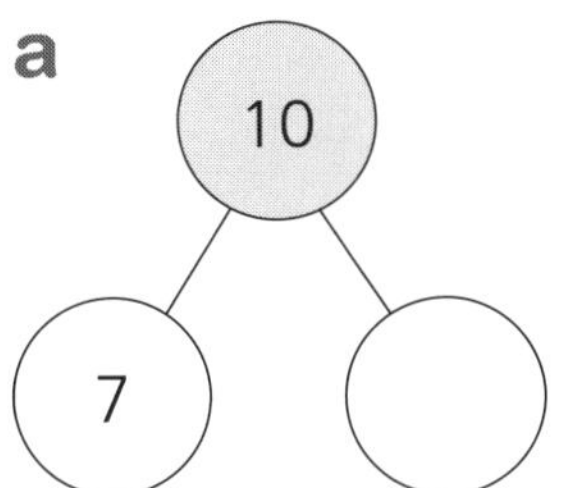

10 – 7 = ____

10 – 3 = ____

7 + 3 = ____

b
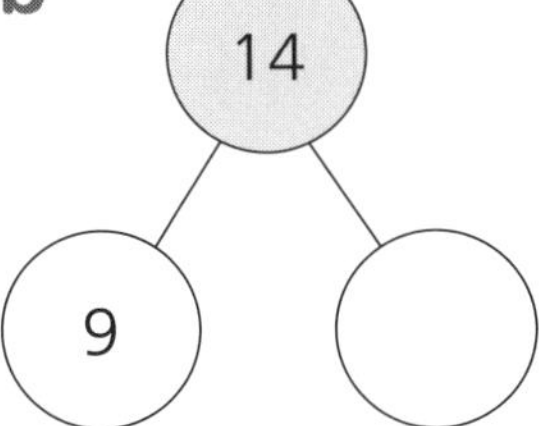

14 – 9 = ____

14 – 5 = ____

9 + 5 = ____

c
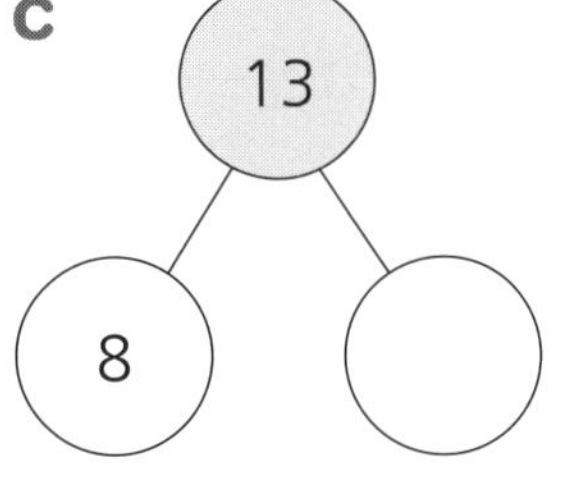

13 – 8 = ____

13 – 5 = ____

8 + 5 = ____

d
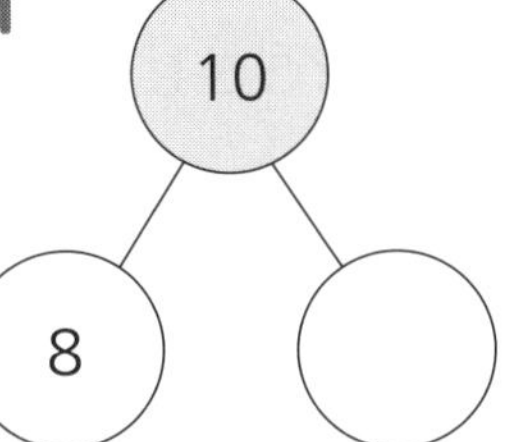

10 – 8 = ____

10 – 2 = ____

8 + 2 = ____

Read this rhyme in your head three times. (Try to learn this rhyme.)

30 days has September, April, June and November. All the rest have 31 except February alone which has 28 days clear and 29 days each leap year.

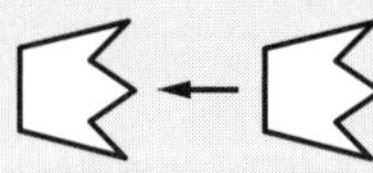 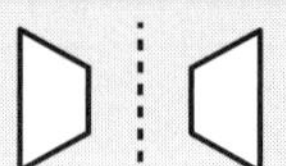

❶ 

6 + _____ = 10 10 – _____ = 6

❷ Fill in the first tens frame, then add the rest in the next.

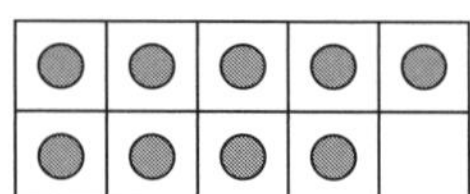 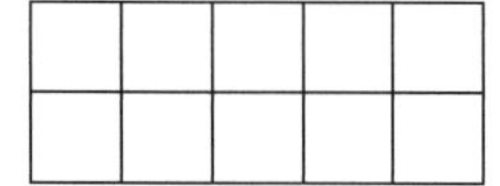

9 + 7 = 9 + 1 + _____

= 10 + _____ = _____

❸  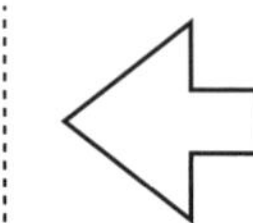

Is this a slide or reflection?

____

❹ Circle the smaller number.

39 or 61

❺ Write a number smaller than 50. ________

❻ Circle the shape on the left.

 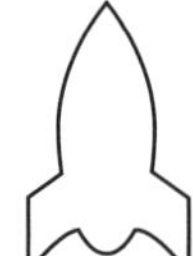

❼ | 9 | tens | 0 | ones | = ________

❽ 7 + _____ = 10 10 + 6 = _____

7 + 9 = _____

Use the number sentences above to find: 16 – 9 = _____

❾ Use the tens frames to find:

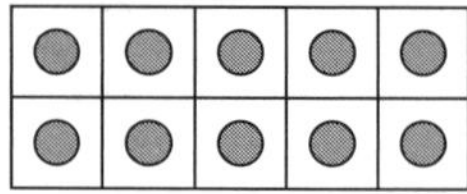 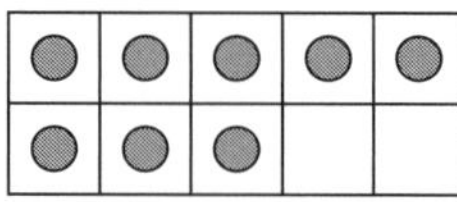

18 + 5 = _____ 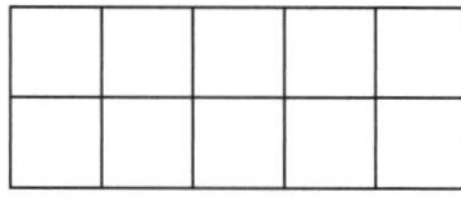

❿ 5 + _____ = 10

⓫ Answer these by bridging to tens.

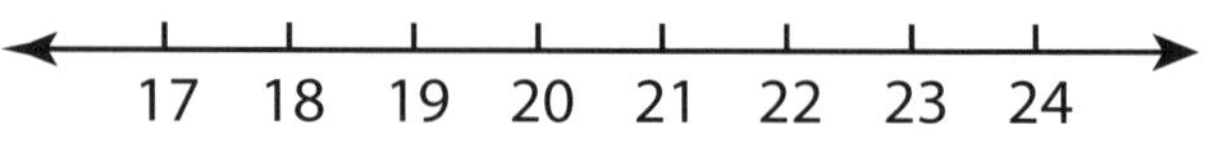

19 + 3 = _____ 18 + 5 = _____

23 – 6 = _____ 24 – 5 = _____

Tick when done.

☐ Practise saying the friends of 10 in your head.

1 + 9 = _____ 2 + 8 = _____

3 + 7 = _____ 4 + 6 = _____

5 + 5 = _____ 6 + 4 = _____

7 + 3 = _____ 8 + 2 = _____

9 + 1 = _____

32:2

25 26 27 28 29 **30** 31 32 33 34 35 36 37

1. Use the number line above to answer these by bridging to tens.

a 31 – 3 = _____ **b** 32 – 4 = _____ **c** 31 – 5 = _____

d 32 – 5 = _____ **e** 33 – 5 = _____ **f** 34 – 6 = _____

2. **a** How many green pencils? _____

b How many yellow pencils? _____

c How many more blue than green? _____

d How many altogether? _____

Tran's coloured pencils	
Red	6 pencils
Blue	8 pencils
Green	4 pencils
Yellow	7 pencils

32:3

5, 10, 15, _____, _____, _____, _____, _____, _____

1. Complete each number bond house.

7	
	1
5	
3	
	2
	4
6	

8	
4	
3	
	5
	2
	1
6	
	7

9	
3	
	4
	1
5	
	2
	8
6	
	7

10	
	9
6	
4	
	1
	5
	3
2	
8	
	7

Multiple-choice questions

Colour the oval next to the correct answer.

❶ This number is:

27

- twenty-two
- twenty-seven
- seventy-two
- thirty-six

❷ What number is shown?

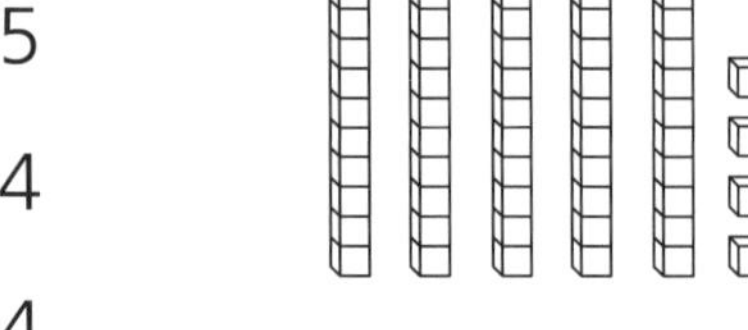

- 46
- 55
- 54
- 24

❸ The number before 40 is:

- 29
- 39
- 41
- 40

❹ The number 3 more than 5 is:

- 7
- 2
- 8
- 6

❺ 12 + 2

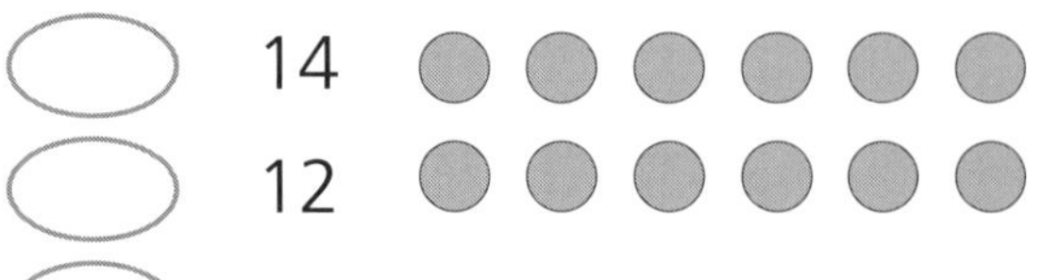

- 14
- 12
- 2
- 10

❻ 5, 15, 25, ______, 45

The missing number in this number pattern is:

- 26
- 35
- 20
- 30

❼ This shape is a:

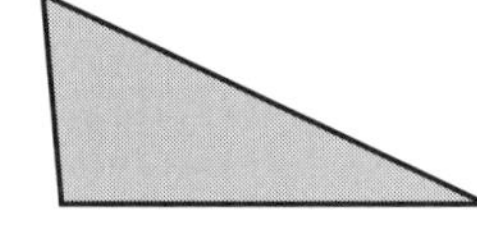

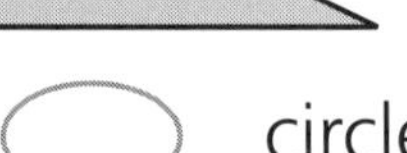

- square
- circle
- hexagon
- triangle

❽ This shape is a:

- square
- circle
- hexagon
- triangle

❾ This 3D object is a:

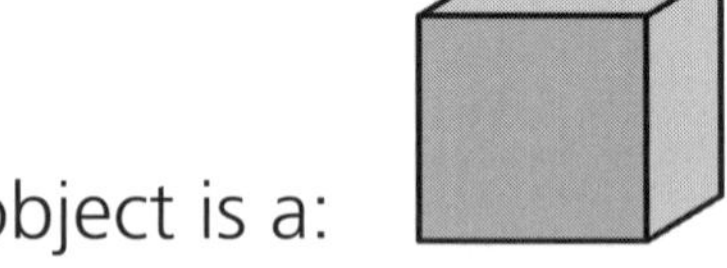

- sphere
- cone
- cube
- cylinder

❿ A cat is heavier than a:

- house
- car
- drink bottle
- man

Hundred chart

Parts of these number charts are covered. Write the missing numbers in the white boxes.

		3		5					
		13				17			
			24				28		30
								39	
			44					49	50
	52			55					
61		63					68		70
				75					
	82								90
	92				96			99	
								109	
			114					119	120

Addition facts to 20

	1	2	3	4	5	6	7	8	9	10
1	2	3	4	5	6	7	8	9	10	11
2	3	4	5	6	7	8	9	10	11	12
3	4	5	6	7	8	9	10	11	12	13
4	5	6	7	8	9	10	11	12	13	14
5	6	7	8	9	10	11	12	13	14	15
6	7	8	9	10	11	12	13	14	15	16
7	8	9	10	11	12	13	14	15	16	17
8	9	10	11	12	13	14	15	16	17	18
9	10	11	12	13	14	15	16	17	18	19
10	11	12	13	14	15	16	17	18	19	20

Checklist:

☐ Memorise your **doubles**.

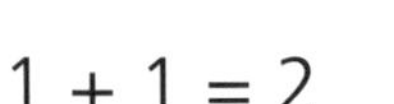

1 + 1 = 2   2 + 2 = 4   3 + 3 = 6   4 + 4 = 8   5 + 5 = 10

6 + 6 = 12   7 + 7 = 14   8 + 8 = 16   9 + 9 = 18   10 + 10 = 20

☐ Learn how to find **near doubles**.

6 + 7 = (6 + 6) + 1 = 12 + 1 = 13   7 + 9 = (7 + 7) + 2

☐ Memorise the **combinations** with answers up to 10.

☐ Learn how to use the **commutative property**.   2 + 5 = 5 + 2

☐ Practise all these addition facts to 20 until you can instantly recall them.

© PEARSON AUSTRALIA 2024 • *AUSTRALIAN SIGNPOST MATHS 1 MENTALS* • ISBN 978 0 6557 0881 0

Number facts: addition to 10

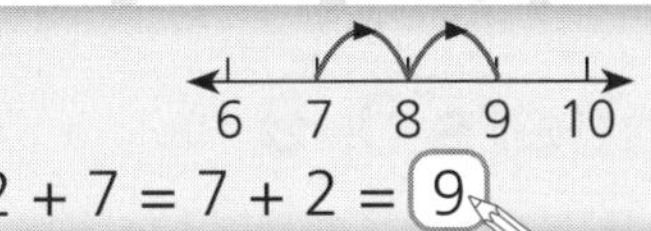

2 + 7 = 7 + 2 = 9

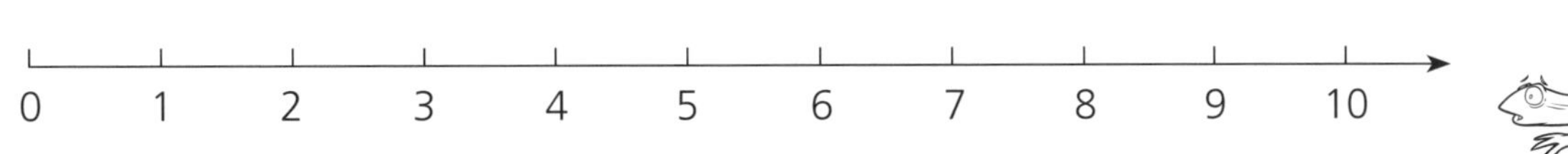

1	2	3
a 5 + 1 = ____	a 3 + 2 = ____	a 3 + 5 = ____
b 4 + 2 = ____	b 1 + 3 = ____	b 4 + 6 = ____
c 3 + 1 = ____	c 2 + 4 = ____	c 5 + 4 = ____
d 2 + 2 = ____	d 3 + 4 = ____	d 1 + 6 = ____
e 1 + 4 = ____	e 4 + 3 = ____	e 2 + 7 = ____
f 3 + 3 = ____	f 2 + 3 = ____	f 3 + 6 = ____
g 2 + 5 = ____	g 1 + 5 = ____	g 1 + 8 = ____
h 6 + 1 = ____	h 4 + 4 = ____	h 3 + 7 = ____
i 1 + 2 = ____	i 5 + 5 = ____	i 4 + 5 = ____
j 4 + 1 = ____	j 5 + 3 = ____	j 1 + 9 = ____
k 5 + 2 = ____	k 6 + 4 = ____	k 6 + 3 = ____
l 1 + 1 = ____	l 2 + 6 = ____	l 5 + 6 = ____
m 2 + 1 = ____	m 1 + 7 = ____	m 2 + 9 = ____
n 6 + 2 = ____	n 2 + 8 = ____	n 6 + 6 = ____

Numbers 0–9

zero zero 0 0 0

one one 1 1 1

two two 2 2 2

three three 3 3 3

four four 4 4 4

five five 5 5 5

six six 6 6 6

seven seven 7 7 7

eight eight 8 8 8

nine nine 9 9 9

© PEARSON AUSTRALIA 2024 • *AUSTRALIAN SIGNPOST MATHS 1 MENTALS* • ISBN 978 0 6557 0881 0

Numbers 10–19

ten ten 10

eleven eleven 11

twelve twelve 12

thirteen thirteen 13

fourteen fourteen 14

fifteen fifteen 15

sixteen sixteen 16

seventeen seventeen 17

eighteen eighteen 18

nineteen nineteen 19

 • *AUSTRALIAN SIGNPOST MATHS 1 MENTALS* • ISBN 978 0 6557 0881 0

Lizards

How would you name each lizard? Find two lizards on each page of this book.

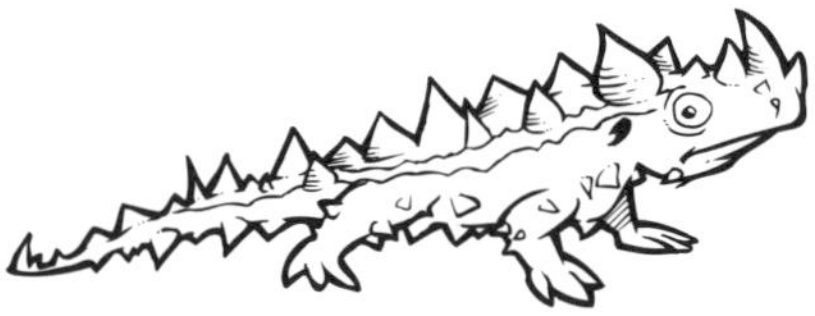

❶

❷

❸

❹

❺

❻

❼

❽

❾

❿

⓫

⓬

⓭

⓮

Real names:

1 Horned lizard **2–3** Bearded dragon **4** Gecko **5** Shingleback lizard
6–11 Common garden lizard **12** Blue-tongue lizard **13** Skink
14 Frilled-neck lizard